IN THE HANDS OF THE
TALIBAN

IN THE HANDS OF THE
TALIBAN
HER EXTRAORDINARY STORY

YVONNE RIDLEY

**ROBSON
BOOKS**

PUBLISHED IN ASSOCIATION WITH
SUNDAY EXPRESS

First published in Great Britain in 2001 by Robson Books, 10 Blenheim Court, Brewery Road, London N7 9NY

A member of the Chrysalis Group plc

In association with
SUNDAY EXPRESS

British Library Cataloguing in Publication Data
A catalogue record for this title is available from the British Library.

ISBN 1 86105 495 5

Typeset by SX Composing DTP, Rayleigh, Essex.
Printed by Mackays of Chatham.

CONTENTS

ACKNOWLEDGEMENTS

There are so many people I wish to thank for enabling me to produce this book, which I dedicate to my wonderful daughter Daisy.

I want to thank my mother Joyce, father Allan and sisters Viv and Jill for their love and encouragement; *Sunday Express* Editor Martin Townsend for giving me the time off to write this book; News Editor Jim Murray and all the staff of the *Sunday Express* for their unstinting support – I'm sorry I put you through so much hell. Special thanks also to Richard Desmond for sending Editorial Director Paul Ashford and lawyer Salaya Hussain-Din to negotiate with the Taliban for my release. Thanks to Jeremy Robson and Joanne Brooks of Robson Books, for their editorial skills and also Andy Armitage. Of course the book could not have been written without my release so the Taliban's one-eyed spiritual leader Mullah Muhammad Omar should be acknowledged along with Abdullah Mounir who protected me when I was held in Jalalabad. Peace and love to the Shelter Now people who kept me sane when I was held in Kabul. There are scores of others who I should also thank who worked behind the scenes to secure my release including James Hunt, Kevin Cahill, John Mappin, Ian Lynch, Julia Hartley Brewer, Helen Carter, Barbara Gunnell, Tracy McVeigh, Rebekah Wade, Anne Graham, Daoud Zaaroura, Joe Mills, Haji Saab, Lone Wolf and Malcolm X. Extra special thanks to my rock and friend Daphne Romney.

1

THE DAY THAT CHANGED THE WORLD

Tuesday 11 September should have been a really pleasant day for me. Although I started the day at the *Sunday Express* newsroom with six weeks' worth of expenses forms to fill in, I was expecting to have a fairly relaxing time. Tuesdays are normally quite civilised days for Sunday newspaper journalists: a day to meet old and new contacts for lunch in the Ivy or Quaglinos followed by some pleasant wine in a local bar and then on to a Soho watering hole.

Unfortunately, however, this Tuesday I had to deal with those expenses forms, a feat that seems to require the mind of an accountant and the memory of an elephant. In the good old days no one questioned expenses or five-hour lunches, but, now that the accountants are steering the running of most national newspapers, things have changed. Pity, because some great stories can emerge during leisurely lunches with story providers.

On top of that I had also promised a good contact that I would visit him in prison following a grave miscarriage of justice. He had been wrongly convicted of perjury – no, not Jeffrey Archer. Someone who really *is* innocent.

Ironically, considering my job as a reporter, I hate working to deadlines. Here I was, at the beginning of the week, with two 'must dos' already. As a result, I was uncharacteristically grumpy and tutted my way through the paperwork. Leisurely lunch? I'd be lucky if I had time to grab a cheese-and-pickle sandwich.

As I was determined not to be distracted, my head was bowed and I was ignoring the usual office banter, which can be quite lively. Various colleagues peeled off, leaving me virtually alone in the office.

Our news operation is part of a small enclave in the major newsroom that houses the *Daily Express* journalists, photographers, newsdesk people, subeditors, graphic artists and other folk who all work to get out the newspaper from an office block on Blackfriars Bridge (known affectionately as 'the grey Lubyanka').

Slowly, in the middle of this fairly unremarkable day, I became aware of people beginning to cluster in front of the TV sets that are strategically placed around the newsroom. I half turned and was shocked to see running pictures of the World Trade Center's north tower on fire.

It was nearly 2 p.m. and I immediately called my elder sister Viv at her flower shop in Newcastle to tell her to switch on the TV. We had been in New York three weeks earlier and she had refused to queue to go up the WTC because she was more interested in a florist's on the ground floor.

I told her the pilot must have had a heart attack or something, and had lost control of the plane, causing it to crash into the WTC. It didn't occur to me that it could be anything else. Later, I cursed myself for not insisting on going up to the observatory.

Viv and I had both fallen in love with the Big Apple and had stayed at the Regent Hotel in Wall Street, where we were treating ourselves to well-earned, five-star, luxury Manhattan style. It was less than two hundred yards away from the WTC and the only five-star-rated hotel in the financial sector. The building was the original stock exchange and had reinvented itself several times since. Now a hotel, it boasts the biggest bath tubs in New York. Pity I just had my big sis to keep me company!

My sister and I had been staying in New York after visiting my eight-year-old daughter Daisy at her summer camp, which was about a two-hour drive away. Daisy was staying there for a total of six weeks. She was entertained every day, had constant care and did not have time to get bored – this was much more fun for her than my hiring an au pair in the UK for the summer holidays. (God, why do I constantly feel the need to justify myself when it comes to Daisy, aged eight, going on 38? She's a fantastic, well-balanced kid and we love each other. I would spend more time with her if I could but the harsh realities of being a single mum and a working journalist make life difficult. Catty remarks from other women certainly don't help, either.)

My memories of New York were in total contrast to the scene that was unfolding before me on TV. Viv was stunned as she listened to my running commentary. Then she hung up to call her husband, Bill Brown, because she knew he had work colleagues in the WTC.

I continued to watch the drama, still totally unaware that American Airlines Flight 11, en route from Boston's Logan Airport to Los Angeles, had been *deliberately* flown into the north tower at 8.48 a.m. New York time.

Around ten minutes later I got straight back on the telephone to my sister. I had just watched United Airlines Flight 175, another Boeing 767, slam into the *south* tower. I was almost hyperventilating as I spoke to her. She immediately hung up and called her husband.

Frustrated, I looked around the newsroom but everyone I needed to speak to was on lunch break. I had to get out to New York. This was terror on an unbelievable scale, the biggest story since the assassination of JFK.

New York City reacted sharply. All bridges and tunnels were closed down and by 2.25 p.m. President George W Bush was describing the WTC strikes as 'an apparent terrorist attack on our country'.

The New York Stock Exchange closed and America's airports had ground to a halt. Someone had gone to war with America and comparisons were already being made to Pearl Harbor.

By now I was running between the TV, the telephone on my desk and my mobile. I tried calling my news editor, Jim Murray, and the editor, Martin Townsend, because I knew I just had to get out to New York.

By 2.45 p.m., American Airlines Flight 77, a Boeing 757, en route from Dulles Airport, had smashed into the Pentagon, causing one of its five sides to collapse. Minutes later the White House was evacuated and we all guessed that it was to be the next target as people talked feverishly about at least one other plane that was unaccounted for.

Damn! I still couldn't get hold of the news editor and I was told to 'calm down' by Jonathan Calvert, an assistant editor, because it was only Tuesday. I couldn't believe it. How could someone remain so calm when the biggest story of the century was unfolding before our very eyes?

I watched in awe as office workers began to hurl themselves from the top floors of the WTC. God, it must have been hellish in there if the only option was to jump out of a high window! I didn't want to watch any more, but I was drawn to the seeming surrealism of it all. It was compulsive viewing, it was happening live and it was horror beyond anyone's wildest imagination.

Jim Murray walked into the newsroom full of bonhomie, followed a few minutes later by Martin Townsend. As I explained what had happened Martin said he wanted to send me to New York, whereas Jim thought I should go to the Middle East, because of its suspected links with the atrocities in the USA.

Personally, I thought I should go to Damascus or Lebanon, where I have some very interesting contacts who could point me in the right direction. After I interviewed Ahmed Jibril, then leader of the Popular Front for the Liberation of Palestine General Command (a group then suspected by some of blowing up Pan Am 103 over

Lockerbie) inside his Damascus bunker in 1992 – while I was seven months pregnant – my standing rose in the more shadowy side of Middle East politics. My standing was also increased by the fact that I was living with Daoud Zaaroura, a colonel with the Palestine Liberation Organisation and a legendary former commander of Fatah Land in South Lebanon from 1972 to 1976, who later became Yasser Arafat's head of intelligence. As the father of my baby-to-be, he moved in with me at my flat in Newcastle and claimed political asylum after Arafat had banned him from continuing our relationship. But that's another story. Anyway, he remains one of my best friends.

Back at the office the editor and Jim threw around all the possibilities and quickly made the decision to send me to New York. As I hurried out of the newsroom the south tower of the World Trade Center collapsed in a plume of ash and debris and, by 3 p.m., United Airlines Flight 93, a Boeing 757 en route from Newark, New Jersey, to San Francisco, crashed just north of the Somerset County Airport, about eighty miles southeast of Pittsburgh.

Off I headed to Heathrow Airport via home to pick up some clothes. By the time I reached the airport, all inbound transatlantic flights were being diverted to Canada and the WTC's north tower had also collapsed.

The scenes were chaotic as I queued at the British Airways desk, only to find out an hour later that there were no flights going over the Atlantic for at least a day. There was a flight to Brazil and I thought I could get that. As I thought out loud, trying to work out the logistics of getting to America, I was told that the borders with Mexico and Canada had been shut. Being a born optimist, I nevertheless bought a flight ticket to New York for Thursday 13 September, because I was convinced the airspace would be open by then.

I headed despondently back to the office with my holdall packed but triumphant that at least I'd got a ticket for New York on Thursday morning. By now, New York's Mayor Rudolph Guiliani had ordered an evacuation of

Manhattan south of Canal Street and I wondered whether the friends I had made some weeks earlier in the 55 Wall Street hotel were OK. I couldn't get through to them – all communications seemed to be down.

I then called Daisy at her boarding school in the Lake District to ask if she had heard the terrible stories of what had happened in New York. Although she had, it was evident that the full scale of those events had not impacted on her. At this point I had the difficult task of telling her that I was going to fly out to New York. I tried to temper the potentially upsetting news by promising her that I would bring her a lovely present back. Having the materialistic tendencies of many children, she was quickly appeased. Daisy and I do a lot of travelling together and she hates my going abroad without her. We always call our trips our little adventures. She reminded me that I must be back in time for her half-term because I had bought tickets for both of us to travel to Amsterdam. Then she put the telephone down – she hates it when I cut off first and always worries whether I'm still on the line during my telephone conversations with her. Still, I think I used to do that as a child.

When I had got back to the office, I had gone across the road to Stamford's Wine Bar and asked for one of Lynne's specials. She's the manager and makes a spectacular Pimm's, probably the best I've ever tasted. I like Stammy's, as it is affectionately known. The banter is good and the girls behind the bar are a laugh, but the atmosphere that night was flat – just bloody awful, in fact. I suppose people everywhere were in a state of shock. From there I ordered a cab to Gerry's Club in Soho.

I usually go home via Gerry's. Actually, I *always* go home via Gerry's! Maybe I should get the taxi to drive in from the top of Dean Street and Oxford Street so I can avoid this nightly temptation. But you tell me where you can go for a drink until 3 a.m., behave badly and run a tab even when you're skint!

I got my membership there by default about eight years before, when I was working as deputy editor of *Wales on Sunday* in Cardiff. I had been in London for some function and bumped into an old mate, an investigative journalist called Kevin Cahill. We'd been to the House of Lords and ended up in Gerry's with three Peers of the Realm. As we made merry, more drink was demanded, but we were running out of funds. Ingenious host Michael said I could become a member if I could find a seconder, and then I could run a tab. At least I think that's what happened! Since then it's been a home from home for me.

I was shocked when I walked in on the night of the 11th, though. It was very quiet, with just a couple at the bar, and they were subdued. We began talking about the day's events and the girl told me it was her boyfriend's birthday – one he'd never forget, I remarked. We reflected about the motives behind the terrorist strike on America and wondered whether it had its roots in the Middle East.

We debated whether this was the start of a huge war of terror on the West and what the backlash would be in London, where we've had to live with terrorist activities for years.

When I got home I switched on my portable TV, which had been behaving very badly lately. However, it flickered into action with the day's events. Some hours earlier, World Trade Center Seven, a 47-storey tower, had collapsed from damage. 200 firemen and 78 policemen were missing. In a speech at Barksdale Air Force Base in Louisiana, President Bush declared that security measures would be taken, and pledged, 'Make no mistake, the United States will hunt down and punish those responsible for these cowardly acts.' Brave, strong and stirring words.

It's a shame that after making his speech in Louisiana he then had to slink off to Nebraska's Offutt Air Force Base, home to the US Strategic Command. I thought he should have made New York his first port of call, and then Washington, followed by Pittsburgh. Although I can be quite critical of our politicians and royalty, I don't think that they would head for the nearest bunker in a disaster.

The next day, I woke up with a hangover and dived into my favourite 'greasy-spoon' café for a latte and bacon sandwich. I read through the newspapers, whose front pages were dramatic and heartbreaking. Once in the office, I worked away on background stories until 2 a.m. We had a huge pull-out to produce and it was a case of 'all hands on deck'.

I made many calls to friends, colleagues and contacts with New York connections, and then I made just as many calls to contacts in the Middle East, some moody characters and just the general sorts of unsavoury types investigative journalists tend to meet. I had to cancel my facial at Harvey Nichols and I never made Chris Boffey's leaving do. He was an assistant editor at the *Sunday Telegraph* and a former *Sunday Mirror* news editor. Chris Hastings, one of his reporters and a personal friend of mine from my days in Newcastle, nagged me about going to the do, and I promised faithfully I would, but by the time I looked at my watch it was after 11 p.m. and I still had loads of work to do.

I can't even keep friends, never mind husbands or boyfriends, I observed wryly. This job can be all-consuming but I never tire of the twists and turns thrown up by life and I tend to believe that old adage that the truth is always far stranger than fiction.

Actually *my life* is stranger than fiction at times. People always give a double take when I say I've been married three times, although Daisy's father was not one of my husbands. I can never understand why it is OK to have adulterous affairs or a series of live-in lovers but not a series of husbands! I guess I have a real appetite for life, what with my relationships and the times I spend at Gerry's. Friends of mine wonder at my energy but I can only sleep about three or four hours, anyway, and I don't like my own company, so I really enjoy going to the club.

I remember being horrified when someone told me that we usually sleep an average of 27 years before we shuffle off this mortal coil. Twenty-seven years! My God, it's frightening! Just think how much you can miss in that time. (In addition to that little gem of information I might add that most people die in their sleep. Ha, so there you go! Now we know why. Going to sleep can prove terminal – so I try to avoid it if I can.)

I got home at three o'clock on Thursday morning. I repacked my holdall and headed for Paddington Station and on to the Heathrow Express for my flight to New York. I would be able to catch up on some sleep during the flight. When I arrived, one of the station's supervisors told me that the service had stopped and would not resume until 5 a.m. As I was about to sit down in the freezing cold station he took pity on me and showed me into a private room, where I crashed out in the corner within minutes. No stamina, Ridley!

He woke me up later and I headed for the Heathrow Express. It was bloody freezing and my padded leather jacket was not protecting me at all. As I arrived in Heathrow I discovered that my flight had been cancelled yet again, so I headed back to the office with the obligatory latte and bacon sandwich being consumed on the hoof.

As America continued to writhe in pain, no journalists in the UK could get out because US airspace remained closed. I did more stories from the office and told Jim, the news editor, that I would have a good chance of getting a flight in the morning because I had purchased a ticket on 11 September, so I would be a priority.

Just then an email pinged on to my screen from my cousin Mikey in Minneapolis. He was devastated and could not comprehend why anyone would want to attack America. I could give him a number of reasons but didn't think it was appropriate. I just wanted to give him a big hug and tell him he was going to be OK, but the truth is things will never be the same again.

I love America and, on the whole, most Americans. I love places where I don't have to queue for fast food and where the service is instant – which rules out most of London. However, I don't think Americans are as resilient as the British and they must be amazed that anyone outside their country could or would dislike them. The Brits have developed quite a thick skin over the centuries. Well, you would, wouldn't you, charging into people's countries with a bible in one hand and a sword in the other? While we have lived with terrorism for thirty years and have developed a sort of devil-may-care attitude, I don't think the average American will ever recover from this.

My cousin and I continued to email each other throughout the day and I felt very sad. Until 11 September, all he had on his mind was his forthcoming wedding day in October.

That evening I left the office at around eight with the city editor, Richard Phillips, and a great pal of mine, Mark Watts, who is now a regular on the business and city news teams.

It was pouring with rain outside, so we decided to bluff a waiting taxi driver that we had called his cab company. Not entirely convinced, he let the three of us in and we were just about to make good our escape when Martin Townsend came bounding down the steps of Ludgate House to jump in his taxi.

As it dawned on us that we had been caught red-handed he called the three of us bandits and said it was nothing less than he expected from the bunch of mavericks he employed. We laughed nervously and at least he offered to drop us off on his way home. We dived out sheepishly in Fleet Street and headed for a pizza and some cheap wine.

Richard said it was a really embarrassing episode and I responded that whenever I put my hand in the cookie jar I always get caught. It was a bit of light relief on what had been a bloody awful day.

After that the guys headed home, I headed for Gerry's, where the atmosphere is good and you can behave as disgracefully as you like and no one will raise an eyebrow.

Friday, the following morning, I was back at Heathrow, where I met a remarkable family of incredibly strong women from the American Midwest. They reminded me so much of my mum, Joyce, and two sisters, Viv and Jill.

They had refused to leave Heathrow Airport on 11 September, even though transatlantic flights had been suspended, and were determined to be the first ones out. They had established a routine of sorts, and airport staff had kept them supplied with pastries and coffee.

I took them for breakfast and asked them if they had enjoyed Britain and what they had seen. Their minds were back home and they were worried for everyone and everyone was worried for them.

Their flight had actually taken off but it had been diverted back to Heathrow once the full scale of 11 September began to filter through. It wasn't until they had reached the airport terminal that they had discovered the real – and horrific – reason for their U-turn.

As I queued for my replacement ticket to New York I began to feel a little uneasy when I heard the airways staff asking how much of a priority it was to fly because they had a lot of Americans to get home. Many of those poor souls came from New York and did not know whether their loved ones were still alive.

My mother called me on my mobile and asked me where I was and whether I had got a ticket. She is always very supportive of my work and, like everyone else, wanted to know what was happening in New York, where I would be staying and what I would be doing.

I assured her I was fine but said if I was out there for a while I would miss Daisy's weekend break starting on 28 September. Mum told me not to worry and said she and Dad would pick her up from the Lake District.

The waiting seemed to take forever but I was about two minutes away when my mobile rang. It was my boss Jim.

I told him that I was minutes away from getting a ticket and I would call him back as soon as I had. His reply stunned me. He told me to forget New York and head to Islamabad instead. I was dumbstruck. All my clothes had been packed for downtown New York, not some bloody souk somewhere in fucking Asia, I felt like saying.

Jim was a bit of an unknown quantity at that point. We had known each other for only a few weeks and we got on very well. He was a total breath of fresh air and had no problems dealing with female reporters, as some news editors do.

But now I was beginning to question his judgment. He quickly detected an air of reluctance but he said that the story was now beginning to develop in Afghanistan and Pakistan and that was the place to be. Still not convinced, I muttered that I would go and find a ticket for Islamabad. British Airways had cancelled flights to the Pakistan capital for that day but someone pointed out that I should try the Emirates airline in the next terminal.

In a very sulky mood, I headed off for the Emirates desk and asked for a ticket to Islamabad. They offered me London to Lahore via Dubai and said I would be better off booking an internal flight from Lahore to Islamabad. I called Jim back and told him I had my ticket. Off I went, still kicking my heels, and boarded the Emirates plane, which was, I have to say, surprisingly luxurious, and so I made myself comfortable and watched an in-flight Bridget Jones movie. I think I preferred the book, but it was enjoyable nonetheless.

I then had several games of chess on the computer screen installed in the headrest in front of me and, by the time I'd finally beaten the computer, we were ready to arrive in Dubai.

I love Dubai. It holds very many pleasant memories for me. During the build-up to the Gulf War, when I was working for the *Sunday Sun* in Newcastle, a photographer, Michael Scott, and I had basically thumbed lifts on RAF Hercules transporter planes around the Middle East.

The plan worked very well and we even kipped on board several of the Royal Fleet Auxiliary vessels cruising the Strait of Hormuz. Everything was fine until our last flight home was cancelled and we were stranded in Dubai.

I still had Husband Number Two's American Express card, and so we used that and spent a great week chilling out in a top hotel until we could bum another free lift on an RAF flight.

I put in an expense claim for about £2000, which nearly gave my editor John McGurk a coronary. 'I just can't pay this, hen. I have not got the money and there's nothing in the budget,' he said. I told him that it would have to be paid and added: 'I used my ex-husband's AMEX card and if you want to tell him that he'll have to foot the bill for my trip to the gulf, that's fine.'

A few days later he found the money after he and his then deputy, Chris Rushton, had scoured through the editorial budget. They spotted a few spare grand in the budget and used that to pay me back. In return, Scotty and I supplied the *Sunday Sun* with acres of picture stories, which lasted right throughout the Gulf War.

McGurk, who went on to work for the *Daily Record* and later at *Scotland on Sunday* as editor, is now an editorial director in Edinburgh for Scotmedia.

But back to 2001, and, by the time I reached Dubai Airport, I was coming round to the idea of Islamabad and perceived it more as an opportunity and a challenge. After all, I loved New York and to see it and its people in so much pain would erase all my happier memories.

Yes, Jim's right, I told myself. Islamabad is the place to be. This is where the next chapter of this horrendous story is waiting to be written into the history books.

Just then my mobile began ringing. It was my mother, Joyce. Imagine her surprise when she had called to ask if I had arrived in New York and I told her where I was. She asked why I was going in the wrong direction and so I told her in a very upbeat manner – my attempt at preventing her from worrying – that I was on my way to Islamabad. I might as well have said I was going to dance with the devil. She went ballistic.

I may be 43 (as the whole world knows now) but she still looks upon me as the baby of the family, her youngest daughter. I tried to calm her down but her motor was running and she was full of hell. Believe me, although she's 73, when Joyce kicks off she's frightening. Whenever I am up to my neck in trouble there's usually a man to blame, and Joyce was gunning for Jim Murray. She was going to ring him up and give him a piece of her mind. He'd as good as sold me to a Russian pimp in her eyes and she thought she would never see me again.

She told me to get on the next plane to London and my dad chipped in that I should get a sensible job and move back home. Although I fully understand her concerns about the type of work I do, I was in fear that my street cred was heading for a cul-de-sac with my new boss. I begged her not to do anything and warned her that if she called the office I would be a complete laughing stock.

I remembered the last time they'd begged me to get a 'proper job'. They had stayed with me for a weekend during the time I was working for the *News of the World*, and I arrived back at 2 a.m. from an S&M party in Harrow dressed in crotchless fishnet tights, a PVC skirt, halter neck, a dog collar and some handcuffs dangling from a spiky belt.

I sneaked in and the kitchen door slowly opened to reveal my mother making a hot chocolate drink. She muttered something about my getting a proper job, something respectable. I informed her – in case she thought I had become a happy hooker – that I was working under-cover for the *News of the World*. She looked at me and said she knew that but she still wished I would get a proper job.

I know I have responsibilities, Daisy in particular, but I love both my job and my daughter, and don't feel that having a child should prevent me from following my vocation. No one seems to understand my job, and that is why it is nigh on impossible for a journalist to have a relationship with anyone outside journalism.

My first husband, Kim, whom I'd known since I was fourteen, looked upon journalism as something of a dirty career, something of which to be ashamed. I'm sure he'd have been much happier had I worked nine to five in an office. When we got married I had just turned down a job in Fleet Street with the *Daily Mail* and taken up a position with the *Northern Echo* instead. Kim's umbilical cord was wrapped around the Tyne Bridge and there was no way he would ever go 'down there'!

Less than a year later the marriage was on the rocks – an eight-year relationship down the pan. Two years later in 1983 I married Jim McIntosh, police sergeant in the regional crime squad. He was very dashing, very exciting and twenty years older than me. He was well into his career, and mine was taking off. By this time I'd moved to the *Newcastle Journal* and then to the *Sunday Sun*, where I got my first taste of reporting for a Sunday newspaper.

Once again, Fleet Street beckoned, but if Kim was welded to the Tyne Bridge then Jim must have been joined at the hip with him. There was 'no way' he would consider a move to London.

I absolutely idolised DS McIntosh, so telling him he was a chauvinist did not really enter into the conversation. Fooling myself, therefore, I spent the next few years pinballing round the regional press and with each move gaining a promotion and more respect in my own back yard. By 1990 Jim and I were poles apart, and then I did the unforgivable: I joined the Territorial Army. In 1992 I met David, Daisy's dad, and we stayed together until 1996. After that, I was married to Ronnie Hermosh, an Israeli, for two years. This split, unlike the one with David, was far from amicable and we are no longer in contact.

I was mentally exhausted from the conversation I'd had with my mother in the middle of Dubai Airport. After closing the line I wandered over to a wonderful seafood counter and ordered some caviar, lobster and blinis with a nice chilled Chardonnay. It was my way of sticking up two fingers to my mother because she hates my 'little extravagances'. I tucked in with sheer delight savouring every drop because I reckoned I wouldn't be doing this once I reached Pakistan.

I have a dislike for hot and spicy food, and I don't eat fruit and vegetables, so I wasn't quite sure what I would be eating for the next few weeks. That reminded me – cigarettes, I must get cigarettes.

Sipping the last drop of wine, I smiled to myself and thought I'd won the battle with Joyce but not necessarily the war. I prayed to God that she wouldn't call the news editor. Could you imagine the humiliation of it all? How long would that little nugget take to reach *Private Eye* or some poisonous little diarist in the broadsheets?

I love my mum and dad but I wish they would stop worrying about me. I wondered whether I would be like that with Daisy when she got older. I doubted it. Daisy is not one of life's chancers: she's a belt-and-braces child and whatever she does in life I can't imagine it will have any risk attached to it. Not that that is necessarily a bad thing. It's horses for courses.

I cast my mind back to when we went to Kenya and we went on a safari. At one stage we came across a giant tortoise being fed on bananas. The owner asked Daisy if she wanted to ride it and she shook her head vigorously. I whispered my favourite encouragement, 'Seize the moment', but she still would not budge.

Eventually the Kenyan picked her up and she sat on the animal's back. Within seconds the look of terror melted away from her face and she started laughing and asked for her picture to be taken. I asked her later why she didn't want to get on the animal's back and she said she thought it might run off with her. We both laughed and I reasserted my beliefs to her: 'You must seize the moment because sometimes we never get a second chance to say yes.'

As the flight took off from Dubai the time difference began to kick in and I dozed off until we reached Lahore. I waited around Lahore for an internal flight and noticed two guys who must be television journos. I could tell from their behaviour and the gear they were carrying. We exchanged pleasantries and they said they were from Czech television and were determined to get into Afghanistan and would try through Peshawar, in northern Pakistan. I wished them well and we all caught a flight to Islamabad.

Once in Islamabad I received a text message to say that Express Newspapers had booked me into the Best Western Hotel and gave me a reference for a care-hire firm. Car hire? I'm one of the world's worst drivers – I give women drivers a bad name – and I was adamant that I would not be driving while I was over here.

A taxi was summoned and off I went to Best Western. I'd been on the go for about 36 hours, apart from all the waiting around at Heathrow. I was in desperate need of a bath and I must have smelled like the inside of a camel driver's jockstrap! I was not in the best of tempers.

The man at the reception desk looked puzzled. He said my reservation had been cancelled and no one was expecting me to turn up. It's probably one of the oldest tricks in the book. Some reporter had turned up out of the blue to check in and found the hotel fully booked, so they must have put in a cancellation call for Yvonne Ridley and – hey presto!

Regardless of the scale or depth of a disaster, some hacks show no regard at all for their fellow journos. It's all about self-preservation and looking after Number One. I remember when the Lockerbie disaster happened in December 1988 that there were all sorts of undignified scenes and infighting going on over hotel-room bookings and bed-and-breakfast reservations.

In particular, there was one *Daily Star* reporter who had taken over a room from a breakfast television presenter who was in a state of shock to discover his suitcase had been repacked and was in the hallway. The hotelier was equally shocked because he had received a call saying the presenter needed to check out quickly shortly before the *Star*'s man arrived.

So, by a similar cheap trick, some bastard had shafted me. I was actually too tired to throw a wobbly, and anyway, before I could, another taxi driver appeared and I was sent to the Marriott, which was also fully booked. It seemed every newspaper and radio and television station around the world had descended on Islamabad.

The Marriott receptionist obviously felt sorry for me – or just wanted me out of his beautiful lobby area quickly since I probably resembled something normally found in the gutter – because he made a few calls and I was sent to the Crown Plaza.

It couldn't have turned out better for me. It was full of journalists from all around the world and none from the UK. I'm afraid I am a bit of an isolationist and have never felt entirely comfortable hunting with the pack. I didn't know anyone and could be left to do my work without interference or having those awkward conversations with fellow hacks who want to know what you are up to.

During my time at the *News of the World* you would never, ever ask the person sitting next to you what they were doing, such was the level of security. It is one of the most professional outfits I have ever worked for, although it has a reputation for making things up, but this is simply not true.

From my own experience there, I discovered the newspaper occasionally holds back 20 per cent of the details on a hatchet story just in case the 'victim' complains or heads for a lawyer. If they do either, the remaining 20 per cent is then usually dolloped out the following week.

From there I moved to the *Sunday Times* and worked with David Leppard, who headed the 'Insight' team for several months, before being offered a contract in the main newsroom. Working with Leppard was a joy, although he is a real secret squirrel and almost paranoid when it comes to protecting contacts. I was full of admiration for his operation and learned a great deal about investigative reporting in my short time with 'Insight'. I could imagine Leppard would be a lone operator in my current circumstances, too.

And so, to bring us back to the Crown Plaza, I was, as I say, delighted to end up there alone. I called the news desk and Jim Murray was pleasant enough. Good, that meant that my mother had restrained herself from making a phone call demanding that he fly me back and put me in charge of a knitting column.

I told him I was sweaty and smelly and really needed a shower. Being a totally relaxed and thoughtful soul, he told me I had loads of time and asked if I would file a two-page spread, around a thousand words – before 3 p.m. That was about three hours away. Talk about hitting the ground running. Aaaaargh!

I began to unpack my Louis Vuitton holdall and noticed that some bastard had cut through the stitching between the zip and the lining. As I took everything out, I could see that only three items were missing: two pairs of my dad's socks (now he'll know why he can never find any, because all the Ridley women raid his sock drawer!) and a half-squeezed tube of toothpaste. The mind boggles.

Anyway, apart from having dog's breath, I took a refreshing shower and emerged wondering what the hell I was going to do. Time was ticking away and the *Sunday Express* was expecting me to file a thousand words in what was now less than two hours.

Great! I was in a strange country. I didn't know anyone other than three hotel receptionists – and wasn't on first-name terms with them. I had nothing appropriate to wear for downtown Islamabad and I was having an exceptionally bad hair day. I should have got my roots done before I left, but when did I have the time? Why, I found myself moaning, don't hairdressers work on Mondays, my only weekday off? It is one of life's great mysteries – that and why men have nipples.

All these inanities were swirling round my head, but I checked them and forced myself to concentrate on the job in hand.

2

THE VIEW FROM JALOZAI

The first thing I needed to do was to get a taxi driver who spoke English. I went back to the receptionist in the Crown Plaza and asked him. A driver was immediately produced and off we went. It rapidly emerged the man could say only 'OK' and thought that this would get him through our journey – blimey, and I thought *I* was a chancer!

Within five minutes we were back at the hotel and I made another polite request for an English-speaking driver. I love Pakistani people because they are so keen to be helpful and, rather than tell you something cannot be done, they try to make things work.

However, the man at the Crown Plaza did deliver this time. Minutes later I was introduced to Pasha, who, within half an hour, became my new best friend. He was fluent in English, had worked all over the world and was extremely amiable. I told him what I wanted and he delivered. Simple, excellent, wonderful Pasha. Pasha had big brown, kind eyes and a roundish face covered by a clipped beard. His jet-black hair was beginning to recede and he looked as if he was about to hit 40. When he laughed he revealed pearly white teeth with a gap at the front. Although not that tall, he played a mean game of basketball but had been laid off for a few days after injuring his knee. Some days I could tell by his limp that he was in real pain but he never complained.

My brief was to speak to some local restaurateur about the impending political crisis over the border and how it was going to ripple through into Pakistan.

We drove off to a small restaurant and there I was introduced to the manager. We sat and drank tea and talked, and talked. Within an hour I had everything I needed to meet my deadline and then it was back to the hotel to phone over the story. It wasn't the most important piece of journalism but it carried the all-important byline – 'Yvonne Ridley in Islamabad'.

Newspaper rivalry is intense, and so naturally we were delighted to discover that the *Mail on Sunday*'s man was still stuck in Abu Dhabi airport after his plane had been delayed and, as a result, he had been unable to file a story. Apparently someone within the *Daily Express* had tipped off the *Mail on Sunday* that we were headed for Islamabad, so they had to play catch-up.

I was told the *MoS* reporter was a dear old friend of mine, Ian Gallagher, and, much as I enjoy being in his company, I hoped he would check into another hotel. Thankfully, when he finally did arrive in Pakistan he headed up to Peshawar and checked into the Pearl Continental.

On the Sunday we visited an Islamic university, which Pasha said was probably the most important madrasa, or religious school, of its kind across the Muslim world. He advised me to wear a traditional dress and headscarf, so we popped into Rawalpindi, where I bought a black pashmina-style shawl. I asked Pasha to keep me right on cultural matters and said that, if I did or said anything offensive to him or anyone else, then he must be brutally honest and tell me, because I had never been to his country before.

I wore a longish black dress and my leather, high-heeled sandals because they were so comfortable.

As we reached the university at Nowshera in the Northwest Frontier Province I saw an unremarkable whitewashed building with a simple domed mosque on one side. It hardly looked like one of the most significant institutions in the Muslim world to me. However, I learned that thousands of olive-skinned, bearded young men graduate every year and 90 per cent head for Afghanistan to see their hero, Osama bin Laden and the Taliban. Bin Laden has an honorary degree from the International Islamic University, known politically as Jammia Haquania.

I'm sure the Americans would call it a school for terrorism, but as far as the teachers are concerned it is a centre of academic excellence on a par with Harvard, Oxford or Cambridge. The eight-year courses cover every aspect of Islamic study and young Muslims throughout the world are drawn to it like a magnet. It is run by Moulana (professor) Sami Ul-Haq, who is chairman of the defence council in Afghanistan and Pakistan and is held in very high regard.

When we arrived he was in Lahore, chairing a meeting of the most senior Muslim clerics in Pakistan and Afghanistan, and, later that night, he was in the company of Pakistan's President Pervez Musharraf, giving advice on the current political climate.

I was taken to a small room, where two young men were sleeping on cushions, and was asked to sit and wait. The moulana's son, Hamid Ul-Haq Haqqani, eventually arrived and we all sat down cross-legged and talked.

Hamid, also a moulana, explained to me that some of the university's most senior tutors had visited bin Laden several times. They all described him as the 'perfect Muslim' because he is regarded as a pious man who has turned his back on the West, Hamid explained. I'm not sure that George Bush or Tony Blair would agree with that, but I continued to listen to this earnest young man.

He said he was very disturbed by American threats of retaliation and denied that his university was run for fanatics and would-be terrorists. He keenly pointed out that everyone was disciplined and there were no weapons in the school, not even knives. He dismissed American

accusations that bin Laden had masterminded the 11
September attacks, which he referred to as a 'mishap'.
Offensive as it may seem to Westerners, most people I
spoke to in Pakistan referred to the atrocities euphemistic-
ally as a mishap.

'Osama bin Laden was an American hero funded by the
Americans when he was fighting the Russians,' Hamid
told me. 'Now they have turned him into an enemy. If this
war of words continues it is going to develop into a Third
World War. This will mean many Muslims, Christians and
Jews are going to be killed.'

It was quite a chilling statement and it was said calmly,
quietly and without passion, which made the hair on the
back of my neck stand up.

As we drove off, I asked Pasha what he thought and he
replied that he was scared for his wife and two young sons
and wondered if he should move them to the countryside.
Like many of Pakistan's 80 million moderate Muslims, he
feared the outbreak of war and was genuinely frightened
about the consequences.

This was before President Musharraf had made his
emotional address to the country, telling his people he
would join in America's war on terrorism and asking for
their understanding and support. The man was caught
between a rock and a hard place but he came over on TV
as a dignified statesman.

The Taliban had warned Pakistan that, if it cooperated
with the West, it would suffer, and a few days later we
were told that four Scud missile launchers positioned at
the Torkham border by the Khyber Pass were pointing in
our direction.

I called my very good friend Paul Beaver, who is also a
military adviser, and expressed some concern. He was
quite dismissive and said that the Scuds would never reach
Islamabad, but warned me to steer clear of Rawalpindi and
Peshawar. I asked him how London was and started to feel
homesick.

I told Pasha I wanted to get into Afghanistan, and so we

resolved to go to the embassy on my first Monday. However, David Leigh, the news editor on the *Daily Express*, laughed at the very idea that I might even get a visa for Afghanistan and said foreign journalists were being kicked out of the country. He asked me to head for the refugee camps instead.

I was hacked off and prattled on to Pasha about male bosses, having two bosses, working for the *Daily* and the *Sunday*. He laughed and was tickled by 'Madam', as he called me.

Still, I was counting my blessings. This Jim Murray bloke seemed to be a really good news editor, I told Pasha, very relaxed and unflappable. He knew how to sell a story in conference – that ritual gathering in newspaper offices attended by the editor and his lieutenants, who earnestly discuss and decide the content of the next issue – and had a very gentle, encouraging manner with the younger members of staff.

His predecessor was very different. We used to be great friends, or so I thought, until he was promoted. I felt his attitude change and I found him difficult to deal with. No one was more delighted than me when he moved on, because after he left I was back on the front page – what a relief!

By the time I'd finished carping on to Pasha, we had arrived at the refugee camps in Peshawar – and some of the sights were heartbreaking. This cold crash into reality put things into perspective and I soon forgot about office politics.

We had an Afghan photographer called Ghaffar Baig with us, whom we had bumped into in Peshawar, and, as tends to happen often in Pakistan, a simple operation takes on the appearance of a convoy. We were soon joined by his colleague Mohammed Riaz from the Dawn Group of Newspapers.

Mohammed had been to England in 1999 and had spent some time working in the *Guardian* and *Observer* offices in Farringdon Road, London. He was very pleasant and seemed to hold influence with camp officials, for which I was grateful.

As we walked through the camp I felt like the Pied Piper. I had the camp officials, Pasha, Ghaffar and Mohammed walking several paces behind me, followed by scores of curious children and anyone else who wanted to join in. When I stopped, they stopped; when I moved, they all moved. In the end I swung around and asked the officials to stop following me. I thought their presence would intimidate anyone I spoke to, but my request was refused.

I told Mohammed this was not what I wanted. I needed to speak to refugees from the past few days and not the ones here who had been installed for ten years or more. He passed on my words to Pasha and Ghaffar, and so we left and headed off for another camp, which we would need permission to enter. I told Pasha that if we asked for permission it would give someone an opportunity to say no, whereas if we went in it would be easier for them to say yes. He loved my logic but said it would get me into trouble.

Mohammed left our party to pick up some travel documents and he said confidently that he expected to get an entry visa for Afghanistan. I envied him.

Anyway, in we went to Jalozai (the largest refugee camp in Pakistan). It was heartbreaking. Some of these Afghans had been living in these squalid conditions for more than twenty years since Afghanistan was first plunged into war.

The homes were made of mud and brick and the newest arrivals from the summer were living in make-shift, canvas tents. The men sat and around and idly chatted while the children played. There was no sign of any women, which is not unusual in this very male-dominated, macho society.

When they do venture out, many wear this all-enveloping blue garment called a burka. It looks stuffy and hot and very uncomfortable. You wouldn't see me dead in anything like that, I thought to myself. Although Western women still suffer at the hands of chauvinists, our life is a blessing by comparison.

I found out later that none of the women make an appearance until around dusk, when they head towards the public toilets and showers. If they are seen during the daytime it is considered immodest.

This really hacked me off. Why is it that women are expected to show full self-control, yet men in any society, East or West, seem to think they have the right to pee any time, anywhere? Can you imagine telling a bunch of men they can't use the toilet until dusk? Can you imagine the outrage? I can see the demonstrations now!

I was trying to work out a delicate way of raising this subject without causing offence, when I suddenly gasped for breath. There, sitting by a fire, poking a stick at a kettle overflowing with scalding water, was a child. She was sitting on her hunkers, grubby knees resting against her flawless, olive-skinned face, which was dominated by saucer-wide brown eyes. A tumble of matted curls hung carelessly around her melancholy features as she played dangerously close to the fire and the kettle.

It was a recipe for disaster, but it wasn't that which caught my breath. This child could have been my Daisy. They were almost identical. I felt the tears well up into my eyes and my throat constrict.

My little girl was sitting in a clean, ironed uniform with all her friends in a school that nestled in the dramatic hills of the Lake District overlooking Lake Windermere in Beatrix Potter country. Every night after playing with her friends she would have a hot bath or shower, maybe even a pillow fight, and go to bed in her dormitory.

Every morning she would get up to a hot breakfast, the laughter of other children and school. Daisy is half Palestinian and her life is very privileged compared with those of other Palestinian children.

This little Afghan girl was sitting in a ragged dress, alone and unhappy. She had no education, no hope and no toys. Her only distraction was a kettle that was threatening to scald her pure olive skin. She didn't know where her next meal was coming from and she was living a hellish existence in a camp of no hope.

Life is so unfair. What had she done to deserve this existence? It's at times like this when you question your faith, regardless of your religion. That image will haunt me for a long time to come.

It's funny how you try to be so professional, and then something happens to give you a swift kick and remind you that you're a parent. I can still feel a lump in my throat when I think of that beautiful child.

As we moved around the camp we managed to communicate with everyone via Ghaffar, who spoke Pushtu, the language of Afghanistan, and then translated in Urdu, an official language of Pakistan, to Pasha, who relayed the words back to me in English. We made a great team and the fact that I was with an Afghan and Pakistani team helped smooth international relations.

Earlier that day we were told a BBC crew had been stoned by some refugees angry at the prospect of an air strike on their country, and two other Western journalists had come under attack. I think the refugees were beginning to feel as though they were on show, like animals in a zoo, and complained about media intrusion. I couldn't really blame them.

I noticed the aid agencies were no longer on site and their offices had been abandoned. Later, I was told they had been urged to quit the camp because none of the Pakistan authorities quite knew how the Afghan refugees would react if and when their homeland was blitzed by American and British bombs. There were fears that the refugees had hidden huge caches of arms around the camp in the event that they wanted to start fighting again.

Afghan men are born fighters and most own a semi-automatic or Kalashnikov by the time they've reached their teens. Fighting is a national pastime and has gone on for centuries either among themselves or would-be interlopers. But I was to find out later that their women are made of even sterner stuff.

There are millions of Afghans living in refugee camps in Pakistan, and Peshawar is regarded in many ways as an extension of Afghanistan. It became obvious to me that backing for an American-British bombing campaign would find little support in this part of the country.

It is a widely known fact that the Afghans are totally ungovernable – probably a bit like the people of the Northwest Frontier Province of Pakistan, who appear to ignore their country's law and liaise instead, reluctantly, with the political agents in the region.

The *Express* foreign editor, Gabriel Milland, called and asked me to file a very emotional colour piece for the daily title, which I was also working for. By the time it reached the paper someone must have changed their mind and a very straight, hard news piece appeared instead. Oh, the frustration of it all!

The following day Pasha and I drove to the Afghan Embassy, where I applied for a visa. To get to the little visa office behind the main building I had to walk into a courtyard area, where a few men sat around looking bemused. I had my head covered by a scarf and my whole body was fully clothed apart from my feet. I was wearing my really comfortable leather sandals, which revealed scarlet-painted toenails.

Despite my attempts to show some respect for their culture the man in the visa office was not impressed and slung my visa application in the direction of a pile of fifty others. I couldn't quite understand what he said after that but I left under the distinct impression the visa would be ready by 9 a.m.

Pasha said that, if I got a visa, then he would take me across to Afghanistan. 'Madam, I cannot let you go out there on your own – you need protecting,' he said.

Our plan that day was to go to a small town in the shadow of the Hindu Kush mountains, where a variety of guns and ammunition are made in a series of illegal lockups and small factories. Children as young as eight are crafting these weapons and so I was greatly excited by this story.

We eventually arrived in Dera-Adam Kheil, which I can only describe as a one-horse town – and it did look a bit like one of those places depicted in Wild West movies, stray goats and Asian influence aside. Pasha and I slipped down a side street and there, in a series of open lockup garages, were men and boys working on eighty-year-old lathes producing a variety of weapons. Pasha spoke to them briefly, explaining what I wanted and who I was. They started laughing and one man, who appeared to be the owner, welcomed me in and we began talking via Pasha.

These people make any sort of gun you require and they were busy churning out Chinese pistols and even used the arms company Norinco's trademark. How cheeky is that! I was offered one for around $60 but I declined, much to the disappointment of the boss man. US dollars are the unofficial second currency in Pakistan, thanks to the black market.

Pasha pulled me aside and said I had made a wise decision because the guns were not reliable and, after they had fired fifty rounds, would be of no use to me. I giggled. Quite why I would want to buy a gun and quite why I would want fire a single shot was beyond me. Yes, I can just picture the expression of the usually blank-faced customs men at Heathrow Airport asking if I had anything to declare. Yes, sir, one pistol. Is that OK?

Pardon the pun, but it's funny how something triggers the memory. Seconds later my mind was in Beirut Airport, 4 January 1997. I had just spent more than a week in Lebanon, a truly splendid place, and as usual I was running late. I dashed through the airport like a maniac with a holdall and my open handbag. I stood impatiently as other passengers went through security checks and their baggage was X-rayed. When it was my turn, luggage and handbag duly went through the X-ray machine and I passed through the security check.

When I reached the other side a Lebanese official had my handbag and asked me if it was mine. I nodded and went to take it. He pulled it back and said, 'Do you recognise this?' He then dipped his hand into my bag and produced a handgun, which dangled menacingly from his little finger.

'I've never seen that gun before in my life,' I protested with wide-eyed innocence. 'Someone must have planted it on me.' Then I thought: I bet he's heard the same protest many times before. My God, I thought, I'm going to end up in prison in Beirut because someone's set me up. What would my friends think? More importantly, what would my mother say? I bet they would all think I was trying to pull off a newspaper stunt, which had backfired.

Just then I heard a woman start to scream and I turned around. She was shouting at me in a very accusing manner and her little son looked on with a peculiar look on his face. The security guard thundered something back at her.

He returned my bag to me and waved me off in dismissive fashion. I was so grateful I didn't remain behind for the outcome and thankfully made my flight with mere minutes to go.

As I queued to board the plane a man who had been following behind me and had witnessed the drama told me I had had a narrow escape. He explained that the young boy had deliberately put the gun in my bag for a joke and when his mother saw the gun she had shouted and accused me of stealing it from her bag.

The mind boggles! What was she doing with a handgun in the first place? But I learned a valuable lesson that day: do not go through airports with your hand luggage or bags open.

Pasha nudged me forward and I was propelled rudely back from my thoughts of Beirut to the Pakistani gun shop. As we walked around, it was explained to me that the metal came from the salvaged hulls of shipwrecks in the south of the country. Once it reached the village it was moulded and pressed into a crude gun shape, and then the men and boys got to work crafting the weapons on the old lathes.

I asked if I could take some pictures and the owner, swatting away the young boys, stood there proudly with his men. When I started asking if I could have the young boys back in the picture the mood changed and Pasha advised me to leave.

'They think you are one of those Christian Aid workers who don't like young boys working for a living,' he explained. How strange, I thought, that a journalist was deemed far preferable to have around than a charity worker. As we left, another man tugged at my sleeve and urged me to cross the main road and look inside his shop.

We went across and he pushed a heavily pregnant goat out of the way of the entrance so we could walk in. There on the wall was row after row of semiautomatics, Kalashnikovs and a variety of hand pistols – all copies but all capable of killing. He then showed me a nasty little weapon that looked like a cigarette lighter but was in fact a crude gun capable of firing a bullet.

Through Pasha, he explained that it was just a mere toy and couldn't really kill anyone unless the would-be killer were at close quarters with his victim. Just then the air was ripped apart by the sound of semiautomatic gunfire and I leaped in the air. Pasha roared with laughter and the man looked at me as though I'd just been beamed down from Mars.

The two men talked and started laughing again. There was more rapid fire outside and I asked what the hell was going on. It transpired that this was just one of the many feudal ruckuses that happen between factions of the tribal people who live in this district, which can only be described as bandit country.

The tribal fights date back generations and are usually started by something trivial. 'They have a saying here that if your hand was your cousin you would cut it off,' confided Pasha in sagelike fashion. I nodded knowingly but I still can't quite work that one out.

Once the 'family row' outside had stopped, we headed out of the door and I noticed some shiny folds of silver paper. I pointed them out to Pasha and he hurried me out of the door. The silver paper contained heroin and was on open sale for anyone to buy. I was slightly irritated that Pasha had more or less frogmarched me towards the car but as we drove off he said, 'You know, madam, sometimes you are sticking your nose into dangerous things and I worry about you.'

I told him I had God on my side – either that or the devil looks after his own. He laughed and said if I wanted to write a story on the heroin trade he would try to organise something. This excited me greatly because Afghanistan and parts of the Northwest Frontier produce the largest amounts of heroin in the world.

Although it is hotly denied by the Taliban, their war machine exists thanks to huge profits from the heroin trade. The leaders probably reconcile themselves with the fact that this evil drug is being smuggled abroad and sold to poison Westerners. Yes, I thought, we will make this our next project.

That night, I returned to the Crown Plaza and filed the copy to Jim and had the photographs developed at a nearby camera shop. The results were fine, so we took them to an Internet place and had them scanned in and sent off to London.

In an ideal world we would have had our own photographer with an electronic camera and the pictures could have been sent immediately. However, this is not an ideal world and you have to be resourceful. Also, and this will infuriate the legions of pals I have on picture desks throughout the UK, I prefer to work alone and hate being responsible for other people.

Many times I have seen good reporters and excellent photographers fall out over the coverage of a story – each blaming the other. I remember really upsetting a bloke called Tony Bartholomew when we visited the Falkland

Islands in 1990 while working for the *Northern Echo*. We were staying with the resident infantry company, the Green Howards, and I introduced Tony as 'my photographer'.

He snarled that I wasn't his photographer and I thought he was being a wee bit precious until a couple of days later he introduced me to one of the officers as 'his caption writer'. Ouch, that hurt. Touché, Tony!

On another occasion, while covering the Tyneside riots in 1991 for the *Sunday Sun*, I arrived at a very hostile scene not far from the Scotswood Road, where police in riot gear and wielding shields were standing at one end of the street and a highly charged crowd were gathered menacingly at the other.

Both sides looked on incredulously as I pulled up slap bang in the middle in my office car with a photographer who had just joined us after spending much of his career in fashion and wildlife. I told him the editor, Chris Rushton, desperately wanted a close-up of someone throwing a petrol bomb. What Chris wanted he usually got – or he would throw a huge wobbly.

The photographer looked concerned, so I explained that we would go over to the public and start chatting to them. I told him not to show any fear and to look them straight in the eye and walk over calmly. The last thing to do, I told him, was make a sharp move, otherwise it could provoke the crowd into doing something silly.

He was still not convinced. We got out of the car and I talked to him calmly. I urged him not to run, otherwise he would become a moving target. There was complete silence and suddenly some stones and bricks began to rain down.

I turned, instructing him not to run, but when I looked he was gone. He was sprinting towards the car and some of the yobs decided target practice was in order. I turned towards the crowd and looked at them again and decided to get the hell out. As I walked briskly towards the car a brick bounced off the bonnet and hit me on the cheek. You can imagine the exchange of words in the car.

I know photography is an exact science, and I don't for one minute think I can produce better results than someone who has trained for years in the art of taking a picture, but the type of work I largely do doesn't require the skill of David Bailey to illustrate the story.

Obviously, I could never do a fashion shoot, cover a riot, take a portrait picture or get anything usable from a sports event, and how they have the guts to leap all over prison vans trying to get 'that' picture of the person inside is beyond me.

Anyway, now that I have managed to alienate and upset every single photographer in the world, I shall continue.

Jim Murray was delighted with the story about the illegal gun factories and asked me to head for Peshawar for a few days because that was where all the militant demonstrations were happening. I decided to keep my room at the Crown Plaza because decent accommodation was becoming as rare as hens' teeth, thanks to the media invasion.

On the way to Peshawar we dropped off to an executive-style housing estate on the outskirts of Rawalpindi to meet General Hamid Gul, the former director general of Pakistan's intelligence service the, ISI. It was a meeting Pasha had organised because he knew the brother of someone's cousin who was married to the nephew of the sister-in-law of General Gul's aunt. No, I couldn't quite work it out either, and was not entirely convinced until the former general called me in person and invited me to his home.

He talked enthusiastically about the Taliban and said he has just returned from Afghanistan after being invited over to see their military parade the previous month. Three hours, he said it took, as the military might of the Taliban was paraded before his eyes.

He listed the tanks, the missiles, the bombs and the strength of the army. He said the young Taliban fighters were rubbing their hands with glee at the thought of

American and British soldiers invading their country. His belief was that Afghans are great fighters and had already repelled the British Army twice during the previous century as well as holding off the Russians for ten years.

I sat there thinking that I was talking to Pakistan's equivalent of Stella Rimmington, the former director general of MI5, and could not imagine her waxing lyrical like this.

Of course you have to remember the ISI was very closely linked to the Taliban and, despite denials from all sides, the regime has received support from the ISI. I mentioned in passing that I wanted to go to Afghanistan but kept meeting a resistance from the people in the embassy. He promised to see what he could do and said he would call them direct because he might be able to oil the wheels for me. Come hell or high water, I knew I would get over the border.

When we arrived in Peshawar all the hotels were fully booked and, on top of that, hotel and bed-and-breakfast prices had risen as much as fourfold. It was ironic that, while New York was, tourist-wise, like a ghost town, the hotel industry in Pakistan was bursting at the seams.

One of the better hotels there was the Pearl Continental and I managed to get myself a room after greasing someone else's palm. There was an arcade attached to the hotel and I noticed a bookshop. As I peered through the window I saw what appeared to be an interesting tome on Afghanistan, and so I decided to investigate further.

I was beaten to the door by a very imposing man who must have scraped in at six foot two, and he went for the same book. Damn! After making his purchase he went off and I discovered he had bought the last copy. The man was none other than the BBC's world-famous John Simpson, whose reports from Afghanistan have moved millions. This was not the last time Simpson was to steal a march on me.

Despite all my self-congratulatory pats on the back over how self-sufficient I was being, the deputy picture editor,

Shawn Russell, contacted me to say the picture quality of the gun factories was crap and asked us to resend them. By this time I had bumped into Ghaffar again and he happily took the picture from me to whack over to London.

That night I walked into the bar on the fifth floor of the Pearl Continental. There, standing before me looking unshaven and unkempt, was my old friend Ian Gallagher and a *Mail on Sunday* photographer. I gave Ian a big hug and told him I felt quite emotional because he was the first Brit I'd spoken to for a week. A couple of other guys shouted over: it was the duo from Czech television whom I'd chatted to at the airport in Lahore.

I asked if they had managed to get into Afghanistan and one waved his hand down and rolled his eyes, but added they were still working on a plan. I smiled and then returned to Ian and asked him how he was doing, and he offered to buy me a drink.

It was a weird bar inasmuch as if you wanted a spirit, you had to buy the *whole* bottle. This concept would go down well in Gerry's, I was sure, but I stuck with a beer.

I was introduced to a couple of guys from the *Sun* and we had a very convivial drink, talking about work and about life in Pakistan, and speculating about what was going to happen in the future. I stuck to the golden rule of journalism and avoided talking about my trip to the gun factory.

On the Friday, 21 September, there was a big demonstration in Peshawar which I went along to with Pasha. I had covered demonstrations before but this one was particularly hostile and I could detect an ugly tension in the air. Fridays are regarded as a holy day among Muslims and this demonstration was being organised by one of the leaders of a religious political party.

Pasha and I stood near to some policemen as the angry crowds marched past. I had my head covered and was wearing clothes that would not offend anyone, but I still felt vulnerable. Pasha whispered to me that he thought we should go and, having been in his company for nearly a week, I began to value and trust his judgment.

I returned to the hotel and spoke with the news editor, Jim. I told him that I did not want to cover any more demonstrations and described this particular one to him. I said my very presence there was causing offence because I was a woman and these are all-male events. I said that it wasn't worth getting beaten up for and he said that was fine and respected my assessment of things.

Just then one of the room managers of the hotel said I had to vacate my room because it had been prebooked to someone else. I checked out but remained on site in the business centre filing copy about the day's events. Pasha said he would organise a bed-and-breakfast for me and urged me not to worry. That man was proving invaluable and took away all the little stressful niggles out of my life.

In the business centre I made the acquaintance of a very nice Irish reporter called Miriam Donohoe, who had been to the Khyber Pass some days earlier. She was the Asia correspondent for the *Irish Times* in Dublin and had been sent from her office in Beijing to Peshawar to cover the impending crisis, conflict or even war.

I told her I wanted to go to the Khyber Pass but she said it was closed to all media. She did, however, have some copy I could crib from her if I needed to. It was a kind gesture and I gave her my email address, but, like anyone else, I wanted to see this place for myself.

Just then the telephone in the business centre rang and she took the call. She was up to her eyes filing copy and asked me if I would speak to a radio station from Bogatá in Colombia. I spoke to a reporter there, who asked who I was and what I was doing and what I thought of the situation after 11 September.

Although I will guard an exclusive with my life, I don't mind helping out colleagues whenever I can, so I started pontificating about President Bush – how he sounded like the sheriff of a local town saying he wanted Osama bin

Laden dead or alive. This was not or should not be the rhetoric of a superpower.

I pointed out that unless America had changed its constitution overnight everyone was presumed innocent until proven guilty – or had Bush held a trial in bin Laden's absence? Basically, I bashed up America, sympathised with President Pervez Musharraf, who I thought had been placed in an impossible position, and said that, out of the 80 million moderate Muslims in Pakistan, the vast majority were against any form of military action in Afghanistan.

Warming to the theme, I went on to say that Musharraf was being bullied by America and Britain into joining the coalition and he was walking a political tightrope that could end his career.

I continued, 'While everyone condemns the events of 11 September, we have to take a step back and think. People are still in a state of shock, many haven't had time to grieve properly and others will never have a body to grieve for. Talk of war and a crusade is entirely inappropriate.' I could hear some Spanish speech in the background but just assumed that I was talking to a bloke in a busy newsroom.

The reporter thanked me and asked me to hold on the line. Minutes later he came back and said the broadcast had been perfect. Oh my God! I thought I had given a fellow journalist an off-the-record briefing when in fact I had just spouted forth to millions of listeners in South America in a live broadcast.

I told Miriam and she laughed. I wandered off into the lounge and there was Jason Burke, chief reporter of the *Observer*. There were big hugs and kisses because we hadn't seen each other for ages. Although Jason was now based at the *Observer*'s offices in London, this was very much his back yard. He had lived in the region, free-lancing, for two years, during which time he was snapped up by the '*Obs*' to be their man covering Asia. Jason and I had met in the 'Insight' office of the *Sunday Times* and when he moved abroad we kept in touch sporadically by email.

It was good to see him and he introduced me to Christina Lamb from the *Sunday Telegraph*. Jason went off and Christina and I sat down together and had dinner – she offered to pay because I was short of Pakistani rupees, although I had my credit card, so I agreed to get her the next dinner. (I'm still waiting to repay the compliment at the time of writing this!) Christina was also to make headlines just a few weeks later when she and photographer Justin Sutcliffe were escorted from their rooms at the Serena Hotel in Quetta by police. She was expelled from Pakistan in November 2001 apparently because she had tried to book an internal flight using the name Osama Bin Laden. She had said in an interview with a local newspaper that she had meant no harm when attempting to book the flight from Quetta to Islamabad at a Pakistan International Airlines office in the south-western city.

We got on very well and gossiped terribly about a torrid affair between two journalists and its consequences. Newsrooms are hotbeds of such gossip and – in spite of my earlier observation that it's almost impossible for a journo to have a relationship with someone who isn't one – I personally usually steer clear of flings with hacks, because, as I learned very early in my career, journalists can be very indiscreet. I suppose it's down to our burning desire to break the news.

Just then our attention was diverted by a John Simpson broadcast. The man-mountain had donned a burka to go off into Afghanistan on an undercover mission. He was placed in the back of an open wagon in the lowliest position because of his new persona as a woman.

It was an outrageously funny broadcast. He is so passionate about his work and so enthusiastic, but I failed to see the point of his story. Maybe I missed the important message but it seemed to me a broadcast about John Simpson wearing a burka to do a broadcast after illegally entering Afghanistan in disguise. Christina and I both laughed and raised our eyebrows, part in admiration and part because it was all so funny.

It planted the seed of an idea in my head. The words 'burka' and 'invisible' began to swirl around and the seed began to grow.

3

CARRYING ON UP THE KHYBER

That night I went up to the fifth-floor bar where alcohol is served to foreign guests only and saw all the familiar faces. Ian Gallagher was there but he left shortly afterwards looking sheepish. That made me nervous because I knew he must have had a good exclusive, unless I was being paranoid – another trait suffered by many journos.

Anyway, I decided not to let it bother me and I began talking to a Spanish-born photographer from New York who had just visited relatives in Israel. He told me that he still had to go home and it was going to be weird seeing the Big Apple without the Twin Towers.

He worked for the New York daily, *News Day*, and he was very pleasant but I could tell he was hurting inside. He was also getting some mild hassle from his girlfriend because they were supposed to go on a holiday and spend some quality time together when he was diverted to Peshawar. I said we were in a difficult profession and unless you worked in this crazy line of business outsiders could not understand.

'But she does work in this business. She's a photographer,' he said, laughing. Just then a Lebanese television reporter walked in and we exchanged pleasantries and names. Tania Mehanna from the Lebanese Broadcasting Corporation was striking to look at and although she appeared to be quite demure, she had a wicked sense of humour. I loved her instantly. She had covered the same demonstration in the morning as I had, and I told her my bottle had gone and I had left.

She then revealed she had been attacked with sticks and a French female journalist had had stones thrown at her. Pasha's instincts, as usual, had been spot on. The three of us decided this called for something a little stronger than a beer, so we bought what looked like a bottle of whisky and drowned out the vile taste with lots of Coke.

I remember someone once telling me there was no such thing as a bad whisky, but, trust me, this stuff was rough. It reminded me of some home-made Irish poteen I had once drunk on an overnight shift at the *Newcastle Journal*. It wasn't called the graveyard shift for nothing and, to amuse ourselves, I and two others began drinking this lethal concoction while filling out the *Times* crossword.

We completely forgot about the time and became so drunk and engrossed in the crossword that we finally called the *Times* switchboard for the answer but the operator refused to end our agony and said we had to buy the paper in the morning like everyone else. I looked at my watch and it was about 5 a.m., so I got a taxi home where Husband Number Two, the policeman, was waiting up. He accused me of having an affair. What a nerve! This coming from a man who eventually left me for another woman.

However, I don't suppose it looked very good coming home reeking of alcohol and insisting I'd been at work but I slurred that he shouldn't judge everyone by his own behaviour. I woke up next morning in the spare room with the hangover from hell.

It was nearly midnight in Islamabad and the three of us were drinking the last of the whisky and Coke. They were great company and we all promised to keep in touch, comrades in adversity, all for one and one for all.

I wobbled over to the elevator and went down to the ground floor, where I had arranged to meet Pasha. I really concentrated on walking in a straight line because I was still very conscious of the fact that alcohol is regarded as offensive to many Muslims.

I got into Pasha's battered yellow taxi and off we went to the bed-and-breakfast he had organised. I remember vaguely going up some flights of stars and being shown into a room with a TV, bed and adjoining bathroom. I quickly crashed out and don't remember a thing until about 6 a.m., when I woke to the thunderous roar of a low-flying jet. It was quickly followed by another and another and I thought: It's started. The bloody war has started and I'm missing it.

I scrambled out of bed and dragged on my clothes from the night before and ran, barefoot, out into the fresh air. I found a fire escape and began climbing upwards as fast as I could. I got on to the roof and to my embarrassment saw the airport – Pasha had booked me into a bed-and-breakfast next to the bloody airport. What I had heard were some early-morning flights zooming overhead. I felt such a fool, but thankfully no one was around to witness this spectacle of Yvonne Ridley still wearing last night's make-up, barefoot and hung over. My descent was more careful as I returned to my room.

After breakfast I told Pasha I wanted to go to the Khyber Pass and he said it was impossible because no foreign journalists were being allowed there.

'You know I can't take no for an answer. I have to see for myself,' I pleaded. He laughed, shook his head with resignation and added, 'OK, madam, we will go. If anyone can get through it will be you.'

We linked up with Ghaffar and went to the political agent's office for the Northwest Frontier, where a very officious civil servant was refusing every journalist's request. It was like the United Nations: Germans, French, Japanese, Czech, Spanish, two Americans and me.

I asked the man very graciously if I could have a travel document that would enable me to travel through the Khyber Pass.

'No journalists are allowed there until further notice. The answer is no.' Those journalists who had already been rejected trooped out while others waited to be told the same.

'Why?' I asked loudly. By this time the official had turned his back on me. He then turned round and repeated that I could not go and I shouldn't waste his time.

'You're obviously not the man who can make decisions around here,' I provoked. 'I want to see your boss. I want to get this from the horse's mouth.'

He looked at me in a very cross fashion and then said something to Pasha. Pasha then replied, and the civil servant said something that was obviously offensive to Pasha, because I've never seen him look so angry.

'Madam, that man has just spoken down to me as though I am uneducated because I don't come from this region. However, you have upset him enough that he is going to see the man above him. He is very angry.'

I told him that coming from Newcastle and having what is known as a Geordie accent often offends the snob class. I'm not sure he understood but he chuckled.

The paper pusher went away and came back. He looked at me as though he'd just found something nasty stuck on his foot and pointed to a door. Pasha and I walked in and there was Shahzada Ziauddin Ali, the deputy chief of protocol for Peshawar, sitting behind a vast desk with flunkies on either side of him.

He asked me why I wanted to go through the Khyber Pass and I said, 'Sir, I am a journalist and my boss has asked me to write a feature on this historic Pass. I fully understand your difficulties and I can see that you are a very understanding man but my boss is not. He will not believe I've been refused entry and he will accuse me of being lazy.

'I've even bought two books on the Khyber Pass, but I

beg you, sir, please let me through so I can do your wonderful country justice by writing and expressing myself in my own words.'

He looked at me very sternly from across his desk, and then, with a hint of a smile, he said, 'You may go, but I warn you that you cannot take any pictures. We will provide an armed escort for you and you must not step out of the car on the journey.'

I thanked him warmly and then I went outside, where all the other foreign journalists were amassed, waiting with bated breath. 'The man says yes,' I beamed. Several journalists punched the air and suddenly the paper pusher was overwhelmed with foreign passports of every nationality. If looks could kill, I would not be writing this now.

'Madam, I don't know how you do it. Sometimes you can be a very hard woman and I get afraid for you, but when you try to be nice you are so charming,' said Pasha admiringly. And he gave one of his infectious giggles.

There was a German TV crew there and I whispered to the cameraman that the deputy political agent had insisted on no cameras. He smiled and said, 'I understand but I cannot be parted from my camera – we are joined together.'

We laughed in a conspiratorial manner and waited for the paperwork to go through.

After an hour – everything has to be done in triplicate and involved visiting another office across town – our motley crew was assembled and our convoy was about to pull off when the strangest thing happened. A Polish man driving a magnificent Japanese touring bike pulled up to get his machine on to a trailer that was joining our convoy.

'Who does he work for?' I asked. Ghaffar, the Afghan photographer who has the habit of appearing and disappearing like a genie in a bottle, told Pasha the guy was a tourist and he had a tourist visa to travel through the Khyber Pass and on to Afghanistan. I made a mental note to try to persuade the Afghan Embassy I was a tourist wanting to spend a weekend in Kabul.

Just as we were about to set off we were joined by a striking young man from the famous Khyber Rifles Regiment. Pasha told me to sit in the front of his taxi for once and I refused. 'There's no way I'm having a man with a loaded gun sitting behind me. *He* can sit in the front.'

The soldier had obviously been told to keep an eye on me, so we both ended up sitting in the back and our convoy set off. As we reached a checkpoint just before the Pass, bundles of official documents were being sifted through, so I stepped outside for a wander.

I saw a big sign saying NO FOREIGNERS BEYOND THIS POINT. Ghaffar shouted over to me that he wanted to take a photo and I stood on one side of the sign while a young boy looked on, perplexed. The picture would be one for the family album, I thought. Little did I realise it would wing its way around the world's media seven days later.

Off we set again for the famous Pass. I was very excited and had been in touch with one of my mates who loiters around Whitehall. He told me to watch out for the regimental crests and said I was in for a great experience.

The famous Pass has been making history for centuries and once again it is in the limelight because of the tension in the region. Military experts are again speculating over its significance. Mighty armies and marauding bandits have all passed through its dramatic gorges and granite crags, along with drug dealers and other smugglers. Even now it is likely that British soldiers will once again march through the Pass, all 53 kilometres (33 miles) of it, which winds around the inhospitable Hindu Kush mountains, northwest through the Safed Koh range, connecting Peshawar and Kabul. It varies in width from 3 to 137 meters (10-450 feet).

From a military point of view it is as strategically important as Gibraltar and Suez because it connects the northern frontier of Pakistan with Afghanistan. The feared Taliban fighters and Osama bin Laden know every nook and cranny, but for strangers this winding passage holds many hidden dangers and is also scarred by tragedy. The Pass has been the gateway for invasions of the Indian subcontinent from the northwest and has had a long and often violent history.

The Khyber Pass is controlled by Pakistan but it had become a no-go area for tourists and media as tension rose in the tribal region over America's expected plans to attack neighbouring Afghanistan.

As we reached the treacherous 3-metre section I could see the German cameraman with his arm dangling from the window of a land cruiser. There, strapped to his wrist, was his massive TV camera, capturing every inch of our journey. The mountains on either side looked unconquerable, although there were a few faint footpaths by precipitous cliffs that had been created over the centuries.

The Pass reaches its highest elevation less than three kilometres (two miles) from the border between Afghanistan and Pakistan, and that was where our convoy stopped and parked up. We looked down at Torkham and it would have been a crime not to take any pictures.

The cameras and videos came tumbling out and the magnificent sight was captured for ever. I looked around for Ghaffar and he had gone AWOL again. Slightly tetchily, I asked Pasha where he was and he went to look for him.

One of the Khyber Rifles explained that we were looking at a strategic gateway dating from 326 BC, when Alexander the Great and his army marched through the Khyber to reach the plains of India.

Later, I read in the copy that Miriam had said I could crib from, that Persian, Mongol and Tatar armies forced their way through the Khyber, bringing Islam with them. Centuries later, when India became part of the British Empire, the British troops defended the Khyber Pass from the British Indian side.

During the Afghan Wars the Pass was the scene of numerous skirmishes between Anglo-Indian soldiers and native Afghans. Particularly well known is the battle of

January 1842 (the last year of the first of the three wars), in which about sixteen thousand British and Indian troops were killed.

The British constructed a road through the Pass in 1879 – during the second war – and converted it into a highway during the 1920s. A railway was also built here in the 1920s but its Afghan side now lies in disrepair. It is such a shame because I bet that that rail journey would be one of the greatest on earth. Damn wars, damn conflicts, damn poverty! Instead of spending money on bombs, wouldn't it be better to feed the world and restore all these magnificent routes and tracks?

Then I saw the many regimental badges hand-carved into the rock by British soldiers and it was very moving.

Just then I caught sight of Ghaffar and went to remonstrate with him. Pasha stood on my toe to shut me up and said, 'Ghaffar has been talking to a friend of his from the Khyber Rifles and I think when the convoy pulls off and turns right we can turn left and head towards Torkham and the border.'

Honestly, Ghaffar is so frustrating, but I could have kissed him then and there. He then took some photographs of me holding a semiautomatic, standing next to one of the soldiers. I gave him my little Nikon camera and he took one of me posing in a very Boadicea-like manner overlooking the Afghan border, wielding a semiautomatic. It was a picture that I was never going to see, but I had no idea at the time.

I am so clumsy that I managed to remove a safety catch after I got part of my scarf caught around the gun. The normally heroic, gutsy Khyber soldiers, who would give anyone a run for their money, scattered in seconds at the sight of me waving this loaded weapon around trying to untangle my scarf.

When I realised what I was doing I froze until one brave soul moved forward and thankfully disarmed me. Everyone laughed nervously, and I have to admit I've seen that expression before when I began my basic training with the

Territorial Army. Little did I know how useful that training was going to be for me less than seven days after this hairy gun-wielding episode in the Khyber Pass.

I joined the TA when I was working in Darlington for the *Northern Echo* in 1990 and, while I have to say that I initially joined for a bet, I ended up really enjoying the experience and the wonderful people I met. The bet arose from a dinner party Jim McIntosh and I held for four of our friends who were, like him, members of the Northumbria Police Force stationed in Sunderland. The conversation was lively and the stories were riveting. There's nothing so funny as real life, and tales emanating from a group of police are gripping, sad, hilarious and compelling.

We moved into the lounge and, although silent, the TV was still on in the corner. Armed with brandies and whiskies, we pondered out loud what we could all do if we weren't in our current jobs. The blokes all said they could fall into security and the girls said nursing because they were already well equipped in first aid and weren't afraid of the sight of blood. Then Margy Rowland, a gutsy copper if ever there was one (she was later invalided out of the force after a vicious assault on her), asked me what I would do.

I thought and thought and the silence was deafening. 'She's bloody useless if you take away her notepaper and pen,' mocked Jim. I was incensed and then my attention was diverted by an army advert looking for TA recruits. 'There you go. I could join the Army,' I declared. They all fell about laughing.

'You wouldn't even make a private in the Pioneer Corps,' sneered Jim. I have to say I was quite peeved but I am good at masking my feelings. I called the 0800 number displayed on the TA advert and left my name and address.

After the weekend the phone went and there was a very nice man from the army on the phone responding to my call. I felt very embarrassed and had, by this time, decided that I really didn't want to join the army. However, as I say, he was a very pleasant man, and so I agreed to pop into the Army careers office in Durham City.

I was wearing a turquoise suit, which I loved until someone pointed out that I looked like a Barclays Bank employee. I reasoned with myself that if Jim thought I was pretty useless then so would the army, and they wouldn't offer me anything. I got such a surprise when I got there because they decided I would be very useful indeed – as a journalist.

'Have you heard of the Territorial Army's Public Information Office? You could become a TAPIO and it carries with it automatic officer rank,' said my man in khaki.

Hmm, I thought, so I wouldn't even make a private in the Pioneer Corps, would I? Right, McIntosh, lesson number one: never challenge a Ridley. I went off for a selection board meeting at the United Kingdom Land Forces HQ in Wiltshire, which was quite intimidating. I had to identify fifty pieces of NATO equipment, give a speech on women soldiers and do a simple report for a newspaper based on facts given to me on a sheet of paper. I achieved the first after spending two days' solid studying all the Jane's defence books in Newcastle Public Library. The second was nerve-racking and the third was a doddle.

When the brown 'On Her Majesty's Service' letter arrived I was gobsmacked to find out I had been accepted. I was to be attached to the Royal Signals in Middlesbrough and begin training immediately. Off I went to collect my kit and when I came back Jim was sitting there with an expression that told me he was not happy. 'The only reason people join the TA is to have affairs.'

I laughed out loud. I could not believe this man. Anyway, undeterred, I sorted through all my kit and prepared to go through my basic training rather than fast-track through Sandhurst Military Academy on a nine-week course.

One of the things you learn is how to handle weapons, dismantle the damned things, clean them, reassemble them and fire them. First, however, we were shown a training video of how things can go wrong and I was appalled at some of the injuries caused by just holding a gun wrongly.

By the time I was given a pistol I was absolutely terrified and shaking. I was taken to a firing range and told to raise my arm if anything went wrong and an instructor would come to my aid. I fired two shots at the target and then the pistol jammed, so I raised my arm and turned round to face everyone.

Suddenly, all these grown men and women soldiers dived to the ground and one instructor shouted at me in a very offensive manner, using not a little Anglo-Saxon, to put down the gun. I did and immediately received the bollocking of my life from the instructor.

'Never ever point a gun at anyone again unless it's the enemy. That fucking gun could have gone off and you could have killed someone,' he bellowed at me as his nose nearly touched mine.

I wanted to be swallowed up by a hole in the ground and vowed never to do that again.

History repeats itself in odd ways, and here I was at the Khyber Pass, once again having men in khaki diving for cover. I was quite embarrassed and decided to walk away from the dramatic viewpoint and towards the road. I bimbled around trying to look as though butter wouldn't melt in my mouth waiting for the moment when Ghaffar, Pasha and I would head for the Torkham border.

Days earlier, there had been tens of thousands of Afghan refugees crowding the border, but Pakistan had put up the shutters and refused them entry. Ghaffar chatted to one driver who had managed to get through and was told that all the refugees had gone and it was deadly quiet as though everyone were waiting for Armageddon.

Our little convoy had pulled itself back together on the

opposite side of the road ready for the journey home. Pasha and I stood firm while Ghaffar remonstrated with one of the soldiers and returned to say the deal had fallen through. Once again my plan to head towards Afghanistan had been thwarted. Still, I was jubilant I had seen the famous Pass and we headed back.

I popped back into the Pearl Continental and saw Ian Gallagher and the photographer in the fifth-floor bar. It was way past our deadlines so it was safe to talk and I asked them what they had been up to. They said they had dressed in traditional Pakistani clothes and had gone to do a story about the guns that were being made at Dera-Adam Kheil.

I gave a start and mentioned that I had been there, too, but two days earlier. We compared notes and it was all very jolly, but I slipped out of the bar and telephoned Jim.

'Look, this is probably a coincidence but the *Mail on Sunday* have done our story on the gun factory. My greatest fear is someone in the *Express* is tipping Dave Dillon [from the *MoS* newsdesk] off about what I'm doing over here. I certainly haven't spoken to anyone, so I know if there *is* a leak it's not coming from here,' I said. For all I know Ian could have had the same conversation with his newsdesk.

That evening we headed back to Islamabad and I told Pasha that David Smith, one of the *Daily Express* reporters, was arriving in town during the early hours of the morning. I had spoken to David the night before and said I would arrange somewhere for him to sleep and I would see that a taxi was waiting for him when he arrived.

He asked me if I wanted anything. 'Toothpaste, please bring me some decent toothpaste. Mine was nicked from my bag and I've bought some Pakistani toothpaste and it's vile – it's so salty.'

Thank God he was arriving, and not just for the toothpaste: it meant I could have a day off and all I intended to do was laze around and do nothing. I arrived back at the hotel looking as though I'd been dragged through a hedge backwards. The reception staff smiled. They were used to seeing me coming and going at very odd hours looking knackered.

In the morning I went down for breakfast and meandered through the buffet. Although I don't like spicy food I had developed a taste for a mild meat curry dish and two fried eggs, the latter to counteract the effects of the former. I was really pleased with myself because I had been in Pakistan for more than a week and I was still functioning normally.

When in Damascus in August 1992, I had ended up with amoebic dysentery and had been seriously ill. I was seven months pregnant with Daisy at the time and had spent three days having round-the-clock care after being flown to Cyprus. I had been advised not to go to Syria because of my condition but I had been trying for more than a year to get an interview with Ahmed Jibril and, when his contacts finally indicated 'yes', I was damned if I was going to say 'no'. It was a 'seize-the-moment' time.

Ahmed Jibril was on America's most-wanted list and so for me it was a very important interview, though subsequently someone else was convicted for the Lockerbie bombing. I had been to Lockerbie on the night of the disaster and I remembered it very clearly – and still do. It had a significant impact on me and affected me badly for many years to come. The flight had been en route from Frankfurt to New York via London when the explosion happened. The final death toll among passengers, crew and people on the ground was 270.

I was working at the *Newcastle Journal*'s head office at the time and had been on the day shift, which ended at 6 p.m. I was about to leave and Wayne Halton, who had just arrived for the graveyard shift, was making some calls to the police, ambulance and fire brigade. He shouted over to the news editor, Tom Patterson, that there had been some sort of plane crash in the borders and we all speculated it would be low-flying RAF jets.

Anyway, I decided to hang round and it rapidly emerged this was something much more horrific. I immediately volunteered to go and Wayne and I jumped in my car and headed off to Lockerbie. It was about 7.20 p.m. on 21 December 1988 and my foot was on the floorboard until we left the A69, headed for Gretna Green. Lockerbie was only fifteen miles northwest, but, as we turned on to the motorway, it was entirely jammed about seven miles down. Deadlines were looming, so, unde-terred, I drove down the hard shoulder and managed to blag my way through every police checkpoint until we arrived, slap bang in the middle of the town.

It was weird. There was a heavy smell of burning aviation fuel in the air and my vision was impaired by a sort of dirty haze. The streets looked as though someone had emptied tons of nuts, bolts and jagged metal from some sort of giant industrial hoover. Townsfolk wandered around glazed and speechless, as if in slow motion.

Wayne went in one direction and I went in another. Apart from a few local Scottish reporters, we were the first newspaper hacks there and we tried to piece together what had happened.

I tried to use one of the local payphones, but it was dead. The budget of a regional newspaper didn't allow for mobile phones, which were, anyway, those huge brick-shaped things in those days, not the slimline gizmos you see today, which weigh but a few grams. I looked around and saw a lorry driver with loads of aerials sticking out of his cab and I asked him if he had a phone. I quickly explained what I wanted and he told me to jump in. Excellent! The *Journal* now had a mobile district office with telephone, and I filed my copy.

As I was reading it out to the copytaker – a typist on the other end of the phone – I mentioned something about a mystery lorry driver who had heroically jackknifed his vehicle across the main road to stop traffic moving forward.

'Hey, that's me,' said my man at the wheel. 'I did that. Are people really calling me a hero? Anyone would have done it.' I returned to the copytaker and said, 'Strike out mystery driver. I'm about to give you a name and address and an account of what happened.'

OK, I was lucky but sometimes you need little breaks like that.

I grabbed Wayne and took him to the cab and he filed his stuff. We had stolen a march on everyone, Tom Patterson was delighted and we worked through the night until the 3 a.m. edition. The way I describe it now may seem callous, but as a journalist you have to try to concentrate on gathering as many facts as possible to give to the reader the next day. You can't break down or get emotional – you have to deliver. Tears are for later and in private.

While there we saw the so-called Rat Pack of national reporters based in Newcastle, including the legendary Clive Crickmer from the *Daily Mirror* and Doug Watson from the *Sun*. Doug, who was in the Arndale Centre doing his Christmas shopping, had been bleeped and had driven up from Manchester. Roger Scott for the *Daily Mail* and Alan Baxter for the *Daily Express*, who had been covering a murder press conference in Sunderland, had also been bleeped. Chris Boffey arrived on a Heathrow-Glasgow flight full of cheer . . . he had been at the *Daily Star* Christmas party and, having a reputation of being able to hold his drink, had been the only one deemed in a fit state to make the journey. I have to say Wayne and I kept out of their way because their huge mobile phones were beginning to run out of juice and we were jealously guarding our secret 'district office'.

It was only during the following days that the full horror and trauma of what happened began to sink in. I suppose now I would be offered counselling, but then it was a naff thing to do. I tried to discuss it with my husband Jim but he was very dismissive. He said he had seen worse in the police force – although I'm not sure quite how he could make that claim! I just stopped talking about it with him.

In truth, I have not been able to enjoy Christmas properly since then, so God knows how the people of Lockerbie cope with it each year. Sometime during the so-called festive season, regardless of where I am, my mind will drift up to that border town, which has been scarred for life. I remember interviewing two parents who had been watching *This Is Your Life* on television. Their two children were playing beneath the Christmas tree when this huge explosion shook their home. Before they could stir a row of aeroplane seats came crashing through their window. Three dead passengers, bodies bloated and burned, were still strapped to them.

That image will live with me for ever. How can you explain it? How did they explain it to their children? The whole experience haunted me and, looking back, I must have suffered from post-traumatic stress disorder – but hard news hacks never talked about namby-pamby things like that. We just carried on.

That is why the Jibril interview was so important to me. I wanted to confront him. I wanted to sort of square off the circle from that night in Lockerbie, and so I had gone to Damascus. If I was expecting a full confession I was going to be disappointed.

He was a mild-mannered man and I think I described him as looking like someone's elderly uncle. His face seemed kind and his deep-brown eyes looked as though they'd seen much pain. We talked through interpreters and he denied being responsible. I asked him three times in different ways but the answer was the same – and you can't really turn round and launch into an aggressive line of questioning with a man who is surrounded by gun-wielding bodyguards.

I decided to try a new tactic and told him about Lockerbie and what I had personally seen: the dead bodies lying littered in the rubble, a child's body stuck on a roof and the townsfolk who had nothing whatsoever to do with

Middle Eastern politics who had been left traumatised. I told him it had also scarred me mentally.

Suddenly the brown eyes narrowed and his face became contorted as he growled, 'We have to pick the bodies of our dead children from rubble daily because of Israeli bombs. Now you have had a taste of what it is like and now you have had a taste of how we suffer.'

Strong words. The hatred was deep and ingrained. There was so much pain and hurt and I left feeling despondent. He did, however, make an offer to meet the Lockerbie investigation team on neutral ground to answer questions about Flight 103, but his offer made through the pages of the *Sunday Sun* in Newcastle and our then sister paper, *Scotland on Sunday*, was never taken up.

I spent several hours in his company and towards the end of the interview I had a searing pain in my gut and was relieved when he bade me farewell. I really don't know how I managed to control myself but by the time I reached my hotel bathroom I was ready to explode.

I couldn't understand why I was so ill because I had been so careful. I had avoided eating salad foods. I had brushed my teeth with bottled water and had avoided ice in my drinks. I writhed in agony for more than a day before I summoned the strength to get to the airport and get out of Damascus and fly to Cyprus. I met with Daoud Zaaroura, the father of my baby, and he took me to a clinic in Nicosia.

The doctor there went through everything I'd eaten and then it dawned on me. I had had a local ice cream, which had tasted absolutely delicious. Yvonne, you stupid bint, I thought. Ice cream is nearly all water. You might as well have drunk from a tap in the local souk.

Ever since my experience in Damascus, I have always been extremely cautious with what I eat, hence, every morning in Islamabad, two fried eggs for breakfast, just in case I needed that binding effect. Although my hotel was very modern, toilet facilities in outlying areas were nonexistent or very basic. I just couldn't imagine dealing with a squatty potty in dire straits and still managing to maintain that vital balance.

As I finished breakfast, David Smith walked in, exhausted after a hellish journey and clasping two tubes of toothpaste. 'Thanks for getting Pasha to pick me up at the airport,' he said. 'I didn't arrive until about 4 a.m.' I was genuinely happy to see him and we hugged. It was good to see someone from friendly territory.

But he couldn't stay long and said he thought he might be heading for Peshawar.

I gave him one of my books on the Khyber Pass and urged him to try to see it because it was such an experience. Fairly young, David's a nice bloke and is a very good writer with a relaxed manner that I would imagine would put many people at ease during an interview. He's also a workaholic – either that or he has no life, because he's always in the office. I know that because I'm often there too!

I told Pasha I would see him the next morning and he could have the day off, but he volunteered to ferry David around instead, which was fine as long as Smithy realised he had to find his own man. Thankfully, I could trust him. He hadn't been tainted by the Fleet Street cynics yet.

I had a lazy day and spent most of it in bed in my room. I was running out of clothes and most of my suitable gear was in the hotel laundry, so I went back to bed wearing an Osama bin Laden T-shirt that Ghaffar had given me earlier in the week.

Throughout the day a hotel employee kept knocking on my door asking whether I needed anything special and whether I was happy with the room service. Honestly, I'd have far more respect for men if they'd just be up front and say, 'Would you like something to drink and can I have a shag?' The answer in this particular case would still have been no but he was becoming particularly tiresome.

I finally fixed him several hours later when I heard the familiar rap on the door. I opened the door and the question was the same, so I replied, 'Yes, there is something special I need. Can you get me a box of tampons? I've just started my period.' Funny, that. Never did hear from him again.

I had met someone some weeks earlier before I'd left for Islamabad and I was quite keen. We kept in touch with text messaging during my time over there and this particular Sunday he sent a message asking how I was. I replied and asked him what he thought of my stories in the *Sunday Express* that day. Obviously fishing for compliments, I waited for the response. It was staggering and read, 'DIDN'T BOTHER BUYING THE PAPER TODAY.' Fortunately for him I was in Islamabad and frankly didn't want to pick up the phone to have a row – it would have been too exhausting. I simply returned the following text: 'BIG MISTAKE'.

He has called me a few times since I returned home but I haven't responded that enthusiastically. He just doesn't understand and most men don't. Newspapers are my life and throughout my life it has been the one, solid, reliable rock that has always been there for me until Daisy was born. Boyfriends and husbands have come and gone and they can't compete with the job.

It provides me with a reasonable income, lots of support, excitement, danger, fun, great lunches, excellent dinners and a network of solid friends and contacts. Daisy gives me unconditional love, so I guess the only thing I'm missing in the morning is a cuddle, good sex and breakfast in bed. And, let's face it, girls, how many of us get *that* every day?

I'm not sure what the male perspective is. I long ago gave up trying to understand men. And it must be quite difficult being a man in the twenty-first century, because women don't like wimps. But they really can't be bothered with macho oiks, either.

No, after three failed marriages I think I'll stick to being a mother and a journalist and try to do justice to both and to the best of my ability. I had dinner recently with a good friend of mine called Barry Atwan, who is editor of *Al-Quds*, the London-based Arabic daily. We sort of mulled over the exes in my life and I reflected: 'You know, I'm probably a prime example of why arranged marriages aren't that bad an idea.' He looked at me seriously for several seconds until he couldn't hold his face straight any longer, and he erupted into uncontrollable laughter.

Barry is one of the few journalists in this world who have interviewed Osama bin Laden, so he is a regular media commentator on the subject and has been in front of the cameras virtually nonstop since 11 September. We first met several months after he had done his world-famous interview with the world's most infamous man.

I was planning to go over to Pakistan and Afghanistan and naturally, like any journo, I wanted *that* interview and wanted some advice and tips. Bin Laden, he said, was extremely cautious and you could not carry anything electronic on your person, or even wear a watch. He said many people would promise me bin Laden but they would fail to deliver and I had to be cautious in my approaches.

I realised it was going to have to be another long-haul project. Ahmed Jibril took nearly a year to get access to and it was quite obvious ObL would take much longer. Still, you know what they say: 'slowly, slowly, catchee monkey'.

I afraid that's another trait I have. I'm not sure whether it's a good or bad quality, but I never ever give up or lose faith if I believe in what I am doing. At the other end of the scale, though, if I think I *can't* do something, I walk away from it rather than fail.

I hate to fail because I hate to feel negative about anything. I don't *do* negative! When I'm down I play this nauseating little game that I picked up from the 1960 Hayley Mills film *Pollyanna*. For those of you who don't know, Pollyanna was an orphan who used to play the Glad Game when she felt sad. Even if something awful happened in her life she would still think of something to be glad about. Pass the sick bags, please! I wonder what

Pollyanna would find to be glad about if she had three broken marriages and countless wrecked relationships? Anyway, at this point my determination to get into Afghanistan and my belief in my job were rock solid. Who knows, I might even achieve my ultimate goal of interviewing Osama bin Laden.

4

DAISY, DAOUD AND DANGER

Pasha arrived early to pick me up and I said it was time to pay another call to the Afghan Embassy in Islamabad. The visa I thought I was going to pick up the other day at 9 a.m. turned out to be Scotch mist. However, I thought I ought to persevere.

I popped my covered head around the door and the visa man looked exasperated. 'I have five hundred visa applications now and they will all be duly processed in Kabul but we are not giving out any just yet. Come back next week,' he sighed.

Undeterred I said, 'I really need to get out to your country and write a balanced account of what's happening. I hear that lots of tribal people are going over the border to give blood at the Afghan hospitals in the event of an American strike. You can have a pint of mine if you'll just give me a visa.'

The offer was met with disbelief and raised eyebrows. I wasn't sure whether he thought I was mad or the offer of an infidel's blood was offensive. Anyway, from the stony-faced response, I could see I was getting nowhere fast.

Pasha giggled when I came back empty-handed. 'You are not invincible. Perhaps you have met your match at last.' I said there was more than one way to skin a cat and we would have to put our heads together for the answer.

We then headed off for a government office where visas are issued for Kashmir, and I submitted an application. I told the official that I had a few days off and wanted to go to the region as a tourist.

'We will let you know in three weeks' time,' he replied curtly after taking my documents. He then walked away and refused to return to the serving hatch, so I left exasperated. I wanted an entry into Kashmir because I knew that was where one of the Al Badr terrorist organisation's training camps was based, which may be bombed by the Americans as a legitimate terrorist target.

I told Pasha of my plans, and we visited several tatty little offices on the outskirts of Islamabad where Al Badr and mujahedin (meaning guerrilla – sometimes spelled 'mujahedeen') organisations were based. Each time I said I was a British journalist and wanted to go to one of the training camps I received strange looks. Pasha intervened and, speaking in Urdu, he explained who and what I was and what I wanted to do.

At least that was what I *think* he was saying! The conversation went on for a long time at one particular office and, judging from their side glances and smiles, I think he told them that I was completely potty but harmless and had good intentions. At the mujahedin office we met a young Pakistani man called Mumtaz, and he said he would try to arrange a trip for me.

We then drove off to a printer's because I needed some business cards produced to replace my London ones, which all bore the *Express*'s familiar Crusader logo. Fearful that the logo would give people the wrong impression, the printer reproduced my card without the famous knight.

The last thing I wanted to do was alienate or offend the Muslims I was dealing with just because President Bush had earlier banged on about a 'crusade' against terrorism. I was fearful of being linked to any anti-Islamic feeling.

It was a scrappy sort of day, so we went off for a coffee to work out what we would be doing that week. 'If the training camps of Kashmir aren't available, the only other thing I can think of is going into Afghanistan,' I said. 'It should make a good story because hundreds of thousands of people are trying to leave and I'd like to talk to the people who are remaining. I want to meet some Afghan women and talk to them. What do you think?'

Pasha made a few phone calls and then handed me his mobile, saying that someone wanted to talk to me. The man on the other end of the line said this could be done for around $1,200 dollars and I would be taken to Daur Baba in Afghanistan.

'You want twelve hundred dollars so I can stick my toe in the border?' I barked. 'I don't think so. Do you really think my head's zipped up at the back? Take me to Jalalabad and around the villages and we have a deal. I'm not going to pay for a silly stunt: I have to go right into the country. Take it or leave it.' I handed the mobile back to Pasha.

Pasha spoke some more to the man and his voice increased in volume. The waiter was looking over in our direction and so was an innocuous-looking Pakistani gentleman sitting behind us reading a newspaper. I glanced back at the stranger and he seemed to be scribbling notes on the paper. I became nervous.

I scribbled my own note to Pasha. It read, 'Lower volume of voice. Possible ISI [Pakistan's intelligence service] behind.' He closed the conversation and we went our separate ways and regrouped at his old yellow car, which may have been battered, with air conditioning that seemed to have a mind of its own, but the engine had the heart of a lion and it did the job. There was no sign of the man in the café, and we headed back to the hotel.

There were a lot of ISI agents hanging around the hotels in Islamabad, monitoring what the media were up to. I swear one of the waiters behind the buffet was a spy – he certainly didn't know one end of a spoon from the other and he looked quite perplexed when asked to do anything more testing than passing a plate.

We had to pass the Afghan Embassy on our way back and I realised there was a press conference on the go, because the streets were lined with TV vans, cars and journos. I decided to pop in, and there was the Taliban ambassador, making his latest statement in the garden. Most of the hacks were sitting on the grass while the cameras were balanced precariously on tripods around the uneven ground.

CNN's chief international correspondent, Christiane Amanpour, was firing questions and trying to be heard while others were also throwing questions at Mullah Abdul Salam Zaeef. Honestly, those guys really needed some marketing advice or spin doctors. I moved round to the right of the garden and stood next to Susumu Arai, the Phnom Penh bureau chief of Japan's daily newspaper, the *Yomiuri Shimbun*. We had met earlier in the day, both pleading for visas to Afghanistan.

Just then a rickety old speaker, perched haphazardly in a tree, dropped out and hit one of his colleagues on the head. Those in our immediate area looked around and saw this dazed and confused reporter rubbing his bonce. I could not resist shouting, 'Look, the first casualty of war!' There were a few sniggers and one of the heavy-turbaned, heavy-bearded Taliban Embassy officials glowered in my direction. He was definitely suffering from a sense-of-humour failure.

The press conference was bizarre and in between statements passages of the Qur'an were relayed to the assembled bunch, who represented probably forty-plus countries from around the world.

Presentation, content and delivery – *nul points*. I felt a tinge of embarrassment for them because they just had no idea how to deal with the media. We could be their greatest asset, I reflected, and yet they just don't know how to use us. I filed some copy to the *Daily Express* foreign editor, Gabriel Milland, because I knew that my *Daily* colleague David Smith was ferreting away in Peshawar.

It had been a fairly scrappy sort of day, so I headed back to the hotel. I spoke to my mother and father and they were fine. Joyce was more relaxed about Islamabad once she realised it was an alcohol-free zone. She hates my drinking and goes mad when my sister Viv tells her I've been quaffing champagne. She just regards it is a complete extravagance and a waste of money. Whenever I go home I tell everyone I'm off to the Betty Ford clinic! No smoking, no drinking and 'eat your greens' and 'have some fruit, it's full of Vitamin C and will do you good'.

She asked about Pasha and she said she wanted to thank him for looking after me and asked if she could speak to him. I mean, how *embarrassing* is that? I bet John Simpson and Kate Adie don't get this sort of hassle!

She asked me what I had planned for the week and I said I didn't really know. Perhaps I would just have a quiet week. Something would emerge, I was sure, I remarked. Naturally I could not, *dare* not, mention that I'd been to the Afghan Embassy three times hassling for a visa; nor could I mention my two projects.

Mums have a sixth sense, though, and mine can smell cabbage boiling in Manchester. 'You just stay away from that Kashmir region or else you'll be kidnapped and we'll never see you. You want to think of Daisy – that bairn needs a mother.' I felt really awkward because I don't like lying to my mum, or anyone else for that matter. Silence was my only option.

As for Daisy, I hadn't even got round to telling her I was in Islamabad because she had been so relieved when she learned that I hadn't gone to New York. She must have wondered, though, why, when I called her every night, I would say I was in bed watching television.

I supposed I was going to have to tell her either tomorrow or the next day because on the Friday she was expecting to spend the weekend with me in London for her exeat. Mum and Dad said they would pick her up and were looking forward to seeing her again. Daisy loves nothing more than pottering around the garden and greenhouse with her granddad and playing with Spot the dog. I hate that dog, well not just that dog, any dog. Any animal that can lick its bottom then try and lick your face is disgusting in my book. I know Daisy's angling for a puppy but hopefully she will grow out of it.

Anyway, that night I sent my news editor an email so he could go into conference on Tuesday morning fully informed of my plans for the week. I told him of my options. It read:

> Hello boss. Went to Al Badr office – they're the ones who have, according to Indian intelligence and CNN training videos, camps in Afghanistan and Kashmir. They want me to go to Lahore for a chat but they are not too hopeful. No Western journalists allowed in for two years. However, I feel they can be persuaded.
>
> Then went to the Hazbul-Mujahdeen office. They also have training camps in Kashmir and are on the new terrorist lists. They insist they are freedom fighters and are keen to talk.
>
> We (Pasha and I) have made friends with a young Mujahedin bloke who says he will escort and smooth our path. Basically if we do either of these routes we are talking at least a day out of Islamabad and if we are successful two days.

I then told him about the plan to go into Afghanistan and added:

> In an ideal world we could probably do both options but this is Pakistan and the word rush or deadline have no meaning. It's like pushing a pram against sludge.
>
> I am up for either option but I will be guided by you. David Smith is in Peshawar at the moment and I filed about eight pars [paragraphs] on a Taliban conference for the *Daily* today –

> voluntarily offered just to keep them sweet
> because we are such nice people on the *Sunday*!
> Still no news of the Afghan visa – they now have
> 500 plus applications.
>
> I heard about a woman who criticised my
> report in the letters page on Sunday. If she is so
> right why are people demonstrating and being
> shot, silly bint.

The last paragraph was in reference to a woman who had
visited Pakistan and said in a letter to the paper that no
one talked about the Taliban and everyone hated the
movement. Apart from being paranoid, journalists can
also be very sensitive souls with fragile egos, so if you
want to get right up their noses send in a letter to their
newspaper.

My email went on:

> According to my man in London nothing will
> happen until the Pope has left and [Jack] Straw
> [the British Foreign Secretary] is back. Friday will
> probably be out because a strike would outrage the
> Muslims on their holy day and encourage people
> to say Bush is launching a crusade. Give my love
> to everyone, Yvonne.

I had been watching CNN before I sent my email and
had seen images of the Pope John Paul II in Kazakhstan.
He had chosen the region now facing potential war to
make a special prayer for Christians and Muslims to live
together without violence. The 81-year-old declared, 'With
all my heart, I beg God to keep the world in peace. We
must not let what has happened lead to a deepening of
divisions. Religion must never be used as a reason for
conflict.'

They were very wise words from a very wise man but I
felt that neither the White House nor Downing Street was
listening, although a crowd of fifty thousand hung on to

every single word as he spoke in Astana's Central Mother of Homeland Square during a Mass.

It was quite surreal watching one of the world's holiest men visiting Kazakhstan, a point where Europe meets Asia and Islam meets Christianity – a neighbour of Afghanistan, home to bin Laden. As the Pope prayed for peace the Western military build-up continued incongruously.

When I spoke to Jim later on he said he had mentioned my plans in conference and said they had been met with a couple of gasps and largely stunned silence. I simply retorted, 'Well it's either of those projects or I sit around and do nothing until the bombs drop and that ain't gonna happen for a week to ten days.

'Even if *you're* happy for me to do that,' I continued, *'I'm* not, because I'll go stir crazy twiddling my thumbs over here. It's a bit light on the old entertainment, although I have an open invitation to the UN Club, where they serve alcohol.

'Have a good think about it. It's only Tuesday and if I go in I'll leave here tomorrow night. We're just going to finalise details in the morning.' He went off to have a further chat with the editor, Martin Townsend. I prayed they wouldn't pull the job.

I was going to go to the UN Club that night and have a few stiff drinks, but I really didn't want to talk to anyone. I was trying to think about what I was doing and what the story was worth. Obviously, there was a risk element, but there's a risk to everything you do. There's a risk to crossing the road, there's a risk to taking a cab, and, as a lot of people found out on 11 September, there's a risk attached to going about trying to live a normal life. Mind you, a story's not worth risking your life for because you simply won't be around to tell it.

Just then the phone rang and it was one of my best pals, Julia Hartley Brewer, political editor of the *Sunday Express* – the one nicknamed GBH. She's a sharing, caring soul and she wanted me to know that she was quaffing my favourite drink – champagne – in the company of the great and the not so great at the Highcliffe Hotel in Bournemouth, where she was covering the Lib Dem conference.

'I know what you're up to, you old slapper,' she teased. 'Sounds a bit risky to me, love. Anyway I know you're somewhere you can't have a decent drink, so I thought I'd have one for you.' We had a good girlie natter and I told her the male tottie was really lacking round the hotel, but I had finally got rid of the 'room service pest' with the old tampon trick. She approved greatly and said she would speak to me later.

Less than thirty seconds later my phone went again and this time it was Tim Shipman, deputy political editor, obviously at a party, too. The things these political people have to do to bring in the news! I said hello and added, 'I've just had your boss on the phone and she's at some bloody champagne soirée and I'm stuck in a country where alcohol's forbidden. Life's not fair.'

Shippers, as he is known to his mates, chipped in: 'I'm at the same party as GBH and she said she'd just spoken to you. You're a totally mad woman. I love you to bits. Best of luck with your story.'

Moments later there was silence. We are operating in two completely different worlds, I thought, then realised I was going to miss out on the annual Labour Party conference. Well, not exactly the conference: it's the networking you have to do at all the fringe functions where copious amounts of booze are thrown into your glass as you mix with other like-minded souls.

I suppose I could go to the UN Club, I pondered – but no: I had a lot on my mind and I had to think everything through in my head. The scales were tipping in favour of Afghanistan and so I sat down and made a few notes. I was going to call Esther Oxford, a fellow journalist who had moved to Islamabad to write a book. We had had dinner together a few evenings ago, after we had bumped into each other at one of the government buildings, and it was really pleasant seeing an old face.

However, I had so much on my mind that I decided not to give her a call because I would have been distracted and not good company. I walked over to the small fridge and took out a bottle of still water. I laughed to myself. I never thought I'd see the day when I'd go into one of those minibars and pull out chilled water – apart from in the morning to soothe a hangover.

My mind wandered back again to Afghanistan and how much of a risk I was really taking. I weighed it all up and it seemed like a good idea. Then I tried to think what other people would do in my position. I thought of a war correspondent friend, Marie Colvin, a true inspiration to journalists everywhere. I bet she would do it. She's got more bottle and guts than anyone I know, and on top of that she writes so well and she carries so much respect.

I first met Marie when we worked on the *Sunday Times* and we would chat when she made her brief appearances at Fortress Wapping, home also to the *News of the World*, the *Sun* and *The Times* (all four are owned by the international newspaper magnate, Rupert Murdoch). Otherwise she would be filing copy that made compulsive reading from the world's many war zones. 'War correspondents will never be out of work,' she recently said and, of course, she is right.

Marie made headlines in April 2001 when she was injured in Sri Lanka after being caught up in a clash between the government forces and Tamil Tiger rebels. The government says the rebels opened fire first when she attempted to cross over from rebel lines in Vavuniva, and the Tamils made counterclaims. The Tamils were telling the truth. She had four shrapnel wounds to her head, chest and arms, but we were all relieved to discover her injuries were not life-threatening. Sadly, Marie lost the sight of her left eye

Sri Lankan officials later said that Marie did have accreditation from the authorities, but had not obtained permission to enter rebel-held territory. However, as I was beginning to find out at the Taliban Embassy, correspondents rarely get permission to cross borders in times of trouble.

Marie later gave the reason for her visit: 'I had travelled through villages in the Vanni and found an unreported humanitarian crisis – people starving, international aid agencies banned from distributing food, no mains electricity, no telephone service, few medicines, no fuel for cars, water pumps or lighting.'

Many say that, if it was not for her investigative reporting, the world would not have known about the plight of the Tamils. Of course, while she was largely praised for her bravery, there were a few snipers in the background saying she had been 'foolhardy'. It is a sad reflection on journalism today, but there is this grudging, humourless section of the media capable only of throwing brickbats.

I have always been inspired by gutsy, professional women. They played an important role in my decision to have my baby. Daisy is probably the best achievement of my life and I am so proud of her; but I remember how shocked I was when I fell pregnant. Daisy is the result of a burst condom and at first I made the decision to have an abortion.

I saw my doctor and then a specialist and basically told them I would cut my throat rather than give birth. I remember the consultant telling me that, at 33, with my body clock ticking away, it might not be possible for me to conceive again.

'Fine, excellent, that's no problem for me. Well, I'll see you next Monday,' I said as I left his office. That weekend I was sent away on a Thomson Regional Newspapers (TRN) training course for women executives, which was set up to find out why women weren't crashing through the glass ceiling.

I was assistant editor of the *Sunday Sun* and had been TRN's first female news editor some years earlier. There were all sorts of women there and they were truly inspirational. I just love good, intelligent female company and these women were all that and more.

As I talked to each one individually I began to realise that having a baby might not be seen as a ball and chain to my career. One senior TRN woman I spoke to was single but her mother, who was in the advanced stages of Alzheimer's, was living with her. She said it was not unusual for her to be called from the newsroom because her mother would be found wandering in the park in her nightclothes.

Another woman, Maureen Simpson, from the Aberdeen TRN papers, had twin teenagers and had just gone through the process of a divorce. But the woman who had the greatest impact on me was an assistant editor at the Edinburgh *Evening News* called Helen Martin.

She was married to a Fleet Street journalist, but shortly after the birth of their baby, they split up. She had discovered that he had been having an affair for over a year. She sold her home and headed back to Glasgow, with about £700, to live with her mother. Starting from scratch, Helen had to rebuild her life, find a job, a home and a nanny for her son to enable her to go back to work and earn money to pay for the last two. I was impressed by her story and how she told it in such a matter-of-a-fact way.

As I travelled home to Newcastle on the Sunday night I reflected on the events of the previous two days and decided, 'To hell with it. I may not be the greatest mother in the world but I am going to have this baby.'

I called the consultant at his home that evening and told him I wouldn't be there in the morning. 'Miss Ridley, I am delighted. I only wish I received more calls like this. I'm sure you will not regret your decision and I feel it is the right one for you.' And, of course, he was absolutely right.

My flatmate Carole Watson gave me a great big hug. She's been a real star, nonjudgmental and very supportive. 'I'm so pleased,' she enthused. 'I just know you're not going to have any regrets.'

I then called Daoud and put him out of his agony by telling him of my decision. He had been devastated when I put the relationship on hold while I tried to sort out this 'pregnancy thing' in my head. In his misery he had applied for a transfer from the Palestine Liberation Organisation's consul in Cyprus to a position in the PLO's Iraqi or Libyan embassy. I guess that must be the Palestinian equivalent of joining the French Foreign Legion!

We had first met the previous summer in 1991, in Nicosia, when I went to visit a South Shields carpenter, Ian Davison, who was serving a life sentence with two other PLO terrorists following the infamous 'siege of Larnaca', in which three suspected Mossad agents were gunned down on board a yacht in the marina in the eighties.

I had been writing to him for nearly three years and he finally agreed that I could visit him, so I arranged to take two weeks' holiday and fly out. I was working for the *Sunday Sun*, which had hardly any budget, so I agreed to pay half the costs.

Although I was in the process of getting a divorce from Jim, my passport still carried his surname, McIntosh. My credit cards were in the name of Ridley and I was staying in an apartment in Paphos, in southwest Cyprus, under another name.

When I arrived in Cyprus I got the last hire car, much to the disappointment of two Englishmen behind me so, I offered them a lift. By the time we arrived in Paphos we were the best of friends. They said they came from Grimsby in northeast Lincolnshire and were in the fish trade, and they had some dealing to do in the northern sector.

I invited them to stay the night in the apartment, which was huge and had three bedrooms. The following morning we drove to Nicosia and I dropped them off. They invited me over to the Turkish sector, and I said I would meet them later in the afternoon in the village of Kyrenia. I then headed for the central prison and filled out the necessary visiting forms for the following day.

Afterwards I went to the PLO consular offices outside the capital and introduced myself. I told their head of media that I was a British journalist called Yvonne Ridley, working for the *Sunday Sun*, a British newspaper, and I wanted to know their opinions of Ian Davison. They asked me to return the next day.

I then went to the checkpoint and crossed over the Green Line and into the Turkish sector with the greatest of ease. I didn't mention I was a journalist because that always gets people overexcited, so I put down my occupation as hairstylist.

In Kyrenia I met the guys from Grimsby and we had a lovely afternoon chatting, sipping wine and eating the most delicious kebabs. I wandered off to a nearby tourist office and began chatting to one of the girls. I mentioned that I was a journalist from the UK and her eyes lit up. She made a telephone call and then turned to me and asked, 'Would you like to meet our Minister of Tourism? He will see you on Thursday. We will have a car to pick you up at the border.' It sounded interesting so I said I would return.

The next day I visited Davison and I saw him virtually every day after that for the remainder of the two weeks. I had also dropped into the British Sovereign bases at Episkopi and Akrotiri to see some friends in the army whom I had met through the TA.

Several days before I left I popped back into the PLO offices and spoke with my contact again. He invited me for some lunch and we went high up the Troodos Mountains and had one of the island's famous mezes.

Afterwards he stopped the car and we went for a walk in the woods. I must say I was feeling a wee bit nervous, especially when I noticed empty gun cartridges scattered on the ground. We were talking about the Palestinian situation and all the time I was looking around for a big stick that I could hit him with if he came near me. Was I going to be taken hostage? Maybe bundled off to Beirut to join Terry Waite?

In the event nothing happened and we returned to the car. However, I have since learned that he had little or nothing to do with the media and was in fact an intelligence officer. He had filed a report saying that he suspected I was a spy of some sort, possibly with Mossad connections. I must say that his report did sound pretty convincing. The PLO had had me followed since the day after I arrived, and in that time they discovered the following:

Yvonne Ridley has entered the country under the name of Yvonne Anne McIntosh. She has checked into an apartment block under another name with two men.

She seems to be able to go to and from the Turkish sector with the greatest of ease and four days after her arrival was picked up by a chauffeur-driven government limousine when she passed into the Turkish sector for the second time. She uses an official ID to get in and out of the British Sovereign bases. A check call to the newsroom of the *Sun* in London reveals that she does not work there. She has a foreign accent which she tries to disguise. She also has no fear characteristic of normal women and appeared calm when she was taken for a long walk through isolated woods.

Of course I could explain each point and there was nothing sinister about my visit. I found it funny that they thought everyone spoke the Queen's English like Her Maj. They had obviously never encountered a Geordie accent before and thought I might be an Israeli.

The file was handed to Colonel Daoud Zaaroura, the head of PLO intelligence. He told Khalid to arrange a meeting and it turned out to be a fateful decision. The moment I first clapped eyes on Daoud I was smitten. The meeting was electric and I was captivated by his charm, totally unaware that I had half of the PLO intelligence section working overtime to find out who I was and what I was up to.

I spent my remaining few days visiting Ian Davison and the nights in the company of Daoud, who, I have to say, was a complete gentleman. He told me he was an investor and I had no reason to disbelieve him. I had no idea I was in the presence of the legendary Abu Hakim, former Commander of Fatah Land in South Lebanon and still revered by many Palestinians today. The Fatah Land was in the southeast of Lebanon and was controlled from 1970–8 by Arafat's Fatah Party.

When I returned to Newcastle I had a cracking exclusive and Tony Frost, the new deputy editor, splashed on the story and promoted it on television. It was a huge success and all my colleagues congratulated me. We went down to the Printer's Pie next to the office and had quite a few drinks.

Daoud and I kept in touch and he visited me some months later at my home in Leazes Terrace, Newcastle. I introduced him to one of my closest friends, Martin Shipton, the investigative reporter with the *Northern Echo*, and they went on to become firm friends.

It was around this time that Daoud dropped the bombshell of who he was and what he did. By then I was a captain in the TA and there was an obvious conflict of interests. I decided not to say anything to my superiors because I wanted to see how the relationship would develop.

I became pregnant in the New Year and went on an army exercise to Cyprus in the April. I was doing 'local boy' stories on a TA regiment that was going out to the Falklands for six months to offer support to the resident infantry company. It was quite an important story because it was one of the first times TA soldiers had been used in full-time positions.

Since I was largely in charge of myself, I was able to nip out of the barracks where I was staying to visit Daoud at his block of flats in the outskirts of Nicosia without having to report to anyone. One night I was resting in his lounge in full British Army kit when Khalid called to see his boss. You can imagine how shocked he was when he saw me sitting there dressed up like Rambo.

He later told Daoud's ex-wife, a Lebanese woman who was closely linked to the PLO. My understanding is that she reported this to Yasser Arafat and said Daoud was in the arms of a Mossad and British secret agent. There was a huge row brewing in the PLO and I thought it was about time I came clean with my commanding officer, a wonderfully charming man called Colonel David McDine.

When I arrived back from Cyprus I popped in to see Colonel McDine and told him I was pregnant and was going to have a baby. He said he was very relaxed about that, as the British Army had developed a more open approach to unmarried mothers. Detecting there was more to come, he winced slightly and said, 'Who is the father. Do we have a problem there? Is it a married officer?'

I replied, 'No, sir. He's not a married officer but there could be a slight problem. He is a colonel but not in the British Army.'

He leaned forward across his desk and said, 'Yvonne, whose army?'

Taking a deep breath, I said the father-to-be was a colonel in the PLO, and he was also head of their intelligence.

Colonel McDine looked at me and said, 'We will have to end this conversation now, Yvonne, and I will make some enquiries to see if this is going to cause problems. Do not talk to anyone about this.'

I got the feeling that he felt matters could have been a lot worse and he was relieved that I had not been messing around 'below ranks'!

It turned out not to be a great problem for me, but back in Cyprus Daoud was ordered to the PLO headquarters, which at that time were in Tunisia. He refused to go, saying our relationship was 'not negotiable'. His wages were cut off, his office telephone was disconnected and a war of attrition developed between Arafat and him. The old man was used to getting his own way and his beloved David, as he referred to him personally, was not towing the line. He came over in the summer and told me about the flak he was getting.

'I have told them we are married,' he said, 'and that we are having a child together and that is the end of the matter. Our story has gone all around the region. It is seen as a big love story and people are amazed.'

It tickled me that I was the talk of the launderette throughout the Middle East. Michael Scott, a trusted friend and photographer, took some 'wedding photographs' of us, which were then shown around Cyprus and Tunisia.

It amazed me that my pursuit of an exclusive interview with a PLO terrorist had created such an impact on so many people's lives, including my own. I really don't go looking for trouble but it seems to find me. I remember Nicholas Hellen, the *Sunday Times* media editor, once telling me I was like journalism's answer to Forrest Gump.

So, here I was in Islamabad, about to set off on another adventure. I knew I was taking a risk but I felt good about the whole operation. I wondered whether I should write some letters to my parents, my sisters and Daisy, my close friends . . . The list was endless, impractical and negative. It was not a Pollyanna thing to do.

There was also the possibility that Martin and Jim might block the project and I even contemplated switching off my phone, an action that could get me the sack. I was determined to see this thing through.

5

MY SILENT WORLD BENEATH THE BURKA

It was nearly midnight. In less than 24 hours I would be in Afghanistan. I spoke briefly to friends and family and my final call was to Daisy. I told her I loved her and she gave me a big kiss down the line.

'Always remember: if you want or need me close your eyes and think of Mummy and I'll be there for you,' I told my daughter. 'You will remember that, won't you, Daisy? I want you to remember this conversation for ever and remember to be very strong.'

My wonderful daughter replied, 'Whatever, Mummy. Now you haven't forgotten my birthday, have you? It's on Wednesday. I have to go now – we're having fun. Bye.'

And with that the line went dead.

I had a restless night's sleep, but that is not unusual for me when I have something weighing on my mind. I knew I could pull the plug on the project if I wanted and if I felt unhappy then I decided I would.

I went downstairs for breakfast and was joined by a lively American photographer who covers Asia for an agency in New York. She was extremely feisty and tough and I would not want to cross her, that's for sure. I didn't tell her what I had planned in case she wanted to join me since, as I explained earlier, I prefer working on my own.

She had lots of pluck and was still covering the mass demonstrations.

After my usual curry and fried eggs, I went to the hotel's business centre and sent the following email to Jim Murray.

Well, I am now fully prepared for my adventure, or as ready as I will ever be. If this comes off then I know there will be pats on the back and if it doesn't I will be called reckless and stupid.

Nothing is safe in this world – as thousands of New Yorkers discovered on September 11. However, there are no Western journalists in Taliban-controlled Afghanistan and we need to get a picture of what is happening inside, even if it is just a snapshot.

I am being very positive and have a strong self-preservation instinct. There are several people who are also risking their lives, so I am not alone. My guide is called Muskeen and he is from the tribal areas on the Northwest Frontier.

We are taking an old, traditional route through the Hindu Kush mountains by four-wheel drive which avoids the Pak border posts. From there we will walk about 10km and then go on horseback to the outskirts of Jalalabad where Bin Laden has a base . . . tho we will be giving that a wide berth. After an overnight stay somewhere we will then head back and I shall file on Friday afternoon.

I have taken every precaution possible. My hair is dyed and so is my skin. I am wearing second-hand, traditional Afghan clothes and shoes. Muskeen will tell people he is going to get his old mother out of the country.

His wife (me) is dumb. We will be armed with semi automatics and will also be accompanied at certain points with armed escorts. Any identification will be left with Pasha at the border.

I was going to write letters to family etc. but that is being negative. I will file on Friday and will contact you as soon as is humanly possible. Can someone stand by to send $2000 dollars once this is all over. That is the fee we have agreed. Those involved know that not a penny will be received until my safe return to Islamabad.

There are some con men in Peshawar who are charging hacks $1200 to take them to the border so they can put a toe in Afghanistan, but this is a nonsense. If we do bump in to anyone during our travels hopefully it will be the boys from Hereford [the SAS] because I'm not sure what will happen if we encounter some men from Fort Taliban!

Looking forward to filing a good feature and hard news story. Love to all.

I then called David Smith, who was in Quetta working for the *Daily Express*. He asked me what I was doing for the *Sunday* and I said, 'Don't even ask. Careless talk costs bylines.'

He replied, 'I can guess what it is. Is this an idea of Murray's?'

I laughed and said, 'No. In fact I know he's having second thoughts about the project but this one's all mine.'

David had gone to Quetta because a refugee crisis of gigantic proportions was beginning to unfold in the south. He said tempers were rising and tension was so high that the hotel most of the journalists were staying in was being protected by armed guards. I thought: If this is what it's like now, what on earth is going to happen when they drop bombs? I told him to be careful and said I would call him towards the end of the week.

Tim Shipman had asked me to keep an eye on David, a close pal of his, because it was his first major assignment, but he didn't need any help. Even if he was nervous on the inside, he oozed confidence and had already found himself an excellent guide.

I hung around the hotel for a while and sent a text message to my man in Whitehall. He said I was mad and urged caution, so I then fired off an email saying I didn't want a lecture: I wanted encouragement. His reply was more positive. I then put in a call in to my friend Paul Beaver, the military adviser, and left a message asking him to call me because I wanted to run an idea past him.

Pasha called to say he would pick me up in the evening and that he was getting his car serviced. I asked him if everything was on course and if everyone was OK about what they had to do and he replied, 'Fine, everyone is fine.'

I went back into the business centre and began reading up on the Taliban.

It soon became obvious to me, after I had checked out a few websites, that the Taliban's aim was to create one of the most fundamentalist Islamic regimes in the world. They certainly didn't sound like fun people and the death penalty seemed to be enforced for the slightest misdemeanour.

Anything associated with jollity appears to be banned unless activities carry a religious theme. So there's no television, no music, no movies; whistling is out, along with dancing, singing, clapping and cheering. Now I am an avid Newcastle United supporter and I just couldn't get through ninety minutes at St James's Park without a lot of the above. It comes naturally, yet it could cost you your life in Afghanistan. It's OK, though, to chant *Allahu akbar* (God is great).

I continued to look down the banned list, which included no smoking, no pork, no recycling the Qur'an, no paper bags (because it might be a recycled Qur'an, I kid you not), no kite flying, no converting from Islam and absolutely *no photography*!

Hmm. Well, I was still going to take my little Nikon camera with me just in case. It was the only piece of equipment I was taking in.

As I continued my search on the Internet, which is also banned, I discovered that some laws applied to men only. There were even rules about beards. Designer stubble and clean-shaven faces would not be tolerated by the Taliban, who insisted that beards had to be long enough for them to protrude from a fist clasped at the point of the chin.

Men who didn't have long enough beards were sent to prison until their facial hair grew to the required length. Men must keep their heads covered at all times and those boys who didn't do the same were denied schooling.

And the laws covering women were ten times as long – funny, that. There's no working outside the home, except in limited circumstances such as medicine and female prisons; no leaving home without a body-covering burka, or without being accompanied by a male relative; no trading or buying in shops where there are men behind the counter.

Education is also denied to women, although I understand that there are many brave females who do run underground schools to educate fellow females.

There were more ridiculous rules, such as the one that says women must not reveal their ankles, and there were some horrendous rules forbidding women to be seen by male doctors.

Cosmetics, of course, were banned, along with laughter, and a woman had to speak in hushed tones lest a stranger should hear her voice. There was no wearing high heels, or anything that makes sound when you're walking. The only sensible ban I saw was for white socks, but that should count for both sexes!

However, the reason for the white-sock ban is also ludicrous. White socks are regarded as a sexual lure. White is also regarded as sacred, because the Taliban flag is a simple white sheet.

Well, I thought, I am really going to have to watch myself

over the border because I could probably break most of those rules within ten minutes. No wonder it is considered an oppressive regime in the West, because all the stories about the Taliban describe their subjugation of women and ethnic minorities.

I went to another website to find out how the Taliban were formed and where they came from. According to one research document, which has largely been accepted by many authors, the Taliban were recognised as a distinct group in 1993, although they didn't rise to prominence until the following year. The Taliban were formed by Mullah Muhammad Omar Akhund, a religious scholar who was 43 years old at the time.

He united a group of around thirty to fifty religious students (the name 'Taliban' means 'student') in a village near the city of Kandahar. According to a report in *Asiaweek* the first Taliban were Afghan youths from refugee camps and madrasas or religious schools in Pakistan's Pashtun belt, which incorporates the Northwest Frontier and Baluchistan. Most of the soldiers came from southern clans of the Pashtun subtribe of Durrani.

Omar's original group were said to be 'united in their anger over the lawlessness into which the Mujahideen [or mujahedin] rule had sunk', said *Asiaweek*. The lawlessness referred to daily extortion at highway tolls, where robbery and rape were everyday occurrences. In July 1994, a Kandahar military leader raped and killed three women, which caused outrage in the city.

Justice from Omar and his Taliban was swift. The leader was executed and his men offered their services to Omar. It was a defining moment for the Taliban, which grew from strength to strength.

Well, I could see that they had started off with the best of intentions but, somehow, I think they have lost their way. Anyway, I didn't intend on meeting or chatting to any Talibs: it was the ordinary Afghans who were my target. I just hoped that I wasn't sussed, because I was aware that if I was discovered, my life would be at great risk. That was fairly obvious.

If I had any doubts about that it was reinforced that evening with Mullah Omar introduced a new ruling that any Afghans giving information to foreigners would be executed. I got the impression he sits down and thinks of new rules every day.

I was feeling hungry, so I went down and headed straight for the hotel buffet, which was fabulous. I really pigged out that night and went back twice. 'I don't know where my next meal is coming from,' I joked with the restaurant manager, who invited me back for more. I was so stuffed I could barely move. I was joined by a Pakistan-born UN doctor, whom I had met earlier in the week. He was a charming man. He told me he had been evacuated from Kabul and he was worried about the offices, hospital and equipment left behind. His main concern was for the people.

I took him into my confidence and told him what I was up to. He was very positive and said I should be well protected by the burka. I explained I had dyed my hair, which was why I was wearing my red Ferrari baseball cap during dinner. I arranged to see him for lunch on Sunday, and we planned to drive out into the countryside so that I could enjoy my visit to Pakistan and could regale him with tales from my adventure. I was looking forward to that.

Having returned to my room, I switched off CNN, because I had overdosed on this phoney war. It was so boring, so many experts predicting what is going to happen – and, of course, as we all know, war is an unpredictable business. However, the one thing everyone was predicting was a humanitarian disaster of spectacular proportions, but the West just seemed to be sweeping this little warning from the aid agencies under the carpet.

I decided to zap through the other television channels, but I have to say, unless you speak Urdu, Hindi or Arabic, the television in Islamabad is dire. My mind immediately switched to Daisy as I saw *Sabrina, the Teenage Witch* with squiggly subtitles. It is her favourite programme but it was so funny to watch the American actors being voiced over by someone speaking Urdu.

Minutes later I pressed the zapper again and I gave a double-take. There was a version of *Who Wants To Be a Millionaire?* in Arabic with Saudi's version of Chris Tarrant and a woman contestant wearing a traditional black outfit revealing only her eyes. I don't know how much money was at stake, but she appeared to be doing very well. Go for it, girl!

I called the office and Jim was seeing the managing editor, Alex Bannister. 'Something to do with your journey and insurance,' said one of my fellow reporters, Keith Perry, a former colleague from my days on the *News of the World*. This industry is so small. We had already thrashed out the plans with the editor and Jim earlier on so I said the only way to communicate with me would be by text message.

Talk of insurance made me feel nervous, so I switched off my phone. What if Bannister throws a wobbly and says I'm not covered and I can't go? I asked myself. I'm mentally prepared for this now, I reasoned; I am psyched up, I can't pull out now.

Then I switched the phone back on and text-messaged my nieces, Victoria and Hollie, to say I had tried to call their Nana but she was engaged. I said I was going to have an early night and I would call her tomorrow. I don't like misleading people but I just couldn't deal with being a barefaced liar to my mother. She has very sharp antennae, anyway, and she would detect something in my voice. That woman knows me better than me – and it's frightening.

Pasha arrived at the hotel for around 8 p.m. and we drove off to a house on the outskirts of the capital, where I was introduced to his delightful wife, two sons and a host of relatives. They didn't speak good English but I pointed out that their English was better than my Urdu.

Pasha said it was necessary for me to change into a traditional Pakistani outfit because we were going right into the tribal area and he didn't want any curious neighbours seeing a Western woman in the area, otherwise it could cause problems for me.

So his wife gave me my first disguise to wear. I went into a room and changed into pastel orange trousers, a turquoise top and an oat-coloured shawl, which covered most of my head. In addition to dying my hair, I had also gelled it back and applied a dark stain on my hands and arms.

Pasha's wife gave me a big hug and he said, 'My wife is very worried about you, madam. She wishes you well and so do all the family.' I turned to thank them and then we jumped in his car.

We met up with Muskeen, my guide, and he did the driving. I have to say his driving scared me and I wondered if I was going to get out of the car alive, never mind get into Afghanistan.

We were stopped several times on the main road to Peshawar by police who made a half-hearted attempt to search the car. My disguise seemed to satisfy them but they were after something else. Money. Apparently the police are so poorly paid that they enforce their own unofficial road tolls.

Muskeen offered one policeman some rupees but he remonstrated with Muskeen and a row developed. Heated words were exchanged and Muskeen grabbed the money back and made a fast getaway. All the men burst out laughing and Pasha explained that the policeman had become greedy and wanted more money. 'Now he has even lost the money he was given in the first place,' Pasha said, laughing.

I started puffing away on my cigarettes – something else that is 'Talibanned', I mused to myself. I kept having to unbutton my yashmak, or veil, so I could smoke.

Smoking is one of the few pleasures in my life and one thing I enjoyed about being in Pakistan is that it's still OK to smoke like a trooper. It would be easier taking crack cocaine than trying to smoke a Benson & Hedges in

London. I work in a nonsmoking office, but I refuse point blank to go outside and join the other smokers. I like to relax and have a fag, not shiver outside as passing motorists sneer. Most black cabs have no-smoking signs and, although it is not illegal, you feel morally obliged not to light up. By the time I leave Ludgate House and dash to Stamford's Wine Bar I'm gasping.

Of course that is something else Mum and Dad hate. I remember when I first smoked a cigarette in front of my dad. I thought he was going to blow a fuse. It was a family gathering and my late Auntie Florence, who enjoyed a cigarette herself, was there. I thought this was as good an opportunity as any to light up, but as soon as my father spotted me he bellowed, 'Put that cigarette out, you hussy.' Well, I never saw Auntie Florence move as fast as she did to stub out her cigarette. Dad's brother, Uncle Tom, turned round and looked at his stunned wife and then looked at me and burst out laughing. Everyone else joined in when they realised Dad had been shouting at me, and of course he had to smile as well. It totally diffused the situation and I carried on smoking.

On the journey towards the Northwest Frontier, we met up with two other men who were apparently going over the border as well. I said to Pasha that I wanted to keep everything simple and he told me not to worry. He introduced me to an English-speaking man called Jan, but I said I didn't want to know any names, as we would keep this on a need-to-know basis.

After midnight we reached a village and drove down a backstreet. A horrible dog was barking. The dogs in Pakistan look lean, mean and downright nasty. I admit I was scared. Thankfully, after much banging, a light went on and the door was opened by a woman in her sixties.

She quietly and gently ushered us inside and she gave me a big hug and a big kiss. These people are so warm-hearted and kind. It is very humbling, and, even though she couldn't speak English, I felt she communicated very well with me.

The men sat outside and talked on camp beds underneath a large moon and a clear night sky. They were smoking and drinking tea and I wanted to join them, but I was ushered into a bedroom, where at least eight other women and a load of children were fast asleep.

A whirring fan was overhead, trying to whisk up some coolness in the stifling heat. The picture immediately reminded me of my favourite wildlife film on the engaging meerkat family. I'm a big fan of meerkats and just love the way they all pull together for what has to be a remarkable display of teamwork. And at the end of the day they are so affectionate that they all cuddle up together.

I was shown to a single bed and had the dubious luxury of a rock-hard pillow. I catnapped for a couple of hours with my surrogate family. When I woke up I was disorientated for a few seconds, then remembered where I was – well, vaguely. I was in someone's house somewhere in the Frontier region.

I looked around and everyone was still fast asleep, and I smiled as a remembered the meerkats again. Daisy would have been very relaxed: she is such a tactile little creature herself. It doesn't matter where we stay, or how many beds or bedrooms there are, she always creeps into mine.

On our first night in Venice, I remember, she jumped into my bed and I said, 'How long are you going to keep this up, sneaking into Mummy's bed?' She laughed sheepishly and said, 'Probably until I'm thirty.' I just rolled my eyes and cuddled her.

By about five o'clock on the morning of Thursday 27 September we were driving towards the border, somewhere in the shadow of that great rampart of mountains known as the Hindu Kush. Muskeen explained to me, through Pasha, that this particular road was frequented by bandits and highwaymen and was not safe to use until daybreak.

We reached a remote farmhouse, still in Pakistan, and a woman in her forties opened the door and welcomed us into a huge courtyard, which was overlooked by a farmhouse. The men went off somewhere and the woman showed me into a small bedroom with a stone floor, and motioned me to lie down and go to sleep.

I had a snooze again but I shot up with panic and fear after feeling something stab my fingers. A small chicken had wandered in from the farmyard and was pecking at me. I'm not sure whether it thought my fingers were tasty morsels or whether it was trying to wake me to get it some food.

The woman entered again and smiled kindly towards me. She pointed to a traditional Afghan dress lying on a sofa and a blue, silk burka. I got changed. And I couldn't believe the change in attitude towards me by the men, even Pasha.

They were pretty dismissive of me and I suddenly went from being a Western woman in charge of a project to someone who had no significance at all. I told Pasha we needed to sit down and discuss the plan again now that we seemed to have extra people on board, but he just told me to get in the car.

We took the road through the Khyber Pass and once again I passed the sign warning that no foreigners were allowed beyond this point. The last time, I had had the authority of the political agent – this time I had none. I didn't even have my passport with me.

By this time we had two cars and we stopped to pick up a woman and two children and her husband. None of them could speak English, so I didn't know what was going on. I had already become invisible and insignificant. The cars stopped and the men went off to a roadside café, leaving me, the woman and her two young children in the back seat.

The windows were shut and I could hardly see anything through the thick lace grille of the burka, which was beginning to feel like a pressure cooker. My head was raging and I could feel sweat trickling down from my head and on to my back.

If I had been a dog in England someone would either have called the RSPCA or bricked the window. I was cursing and swearing under my breath. For half an hour we were left to bake in that bloody car. I was almost hyperventilating. What I wanted to do was leap out and go over to the men and ask what the hell was going on but that certainly would have blown my cover. Then I remembered one of the flaming Taliban rules about not raising your voice.

Just then, the men returned and we set off again. I said loudly to Pasha through gritted teeth, 'Why have we got half the members of the Von Trapp family travelling with us? What the hell is going on?'

He asked me what I was talking about and I hissed, 'Von Trapp, the Swiss Family Robinson, the Waltons, whatever you like. What happened to "let's keep things simple"?'

He just said, 'Don't worry, madam. You are now part of a wedding party going into Afghanistan. It will work much better.'

Before I could add much more, we had stopped and for some reason we had changed drivers. We drove past the spot where I had nearly shot half a dozen members of the Khyber Rifles and in less than ten minutes we were at the Torkham border.

We got out of the car and I lifted my burka to a cowl shape and said to Pasha, 'I don't like this. This is not what we planned—' But I was stopped in my tracks by his sharp words: 'Shut up. Cover your face – there's a Talib coming.'

I almost froze with fear and did as I was told. Then the woman gave me one of her children to carry and she gently but firmly guided me towards the border. Shit, shit, shit! I was petrified. As I walked towards a Taliban checkpoint with the two men, the woman and the children a man began shouting at me in Pashtun.

I haven't even got into Afghanistan, I thought, and they've sussed me already. I gently turned around and it was a medical checkpoint, where children were being given some sort of UN vaccine before entering the country. Maybe it was for smallpox or something.

Thankfully, the woman took the lead and she went with her child, and so I followed. The doctor said something to me and I vaguely nodded as he put a couple of drops of the vaccine into the child's mouth. We then walked back to the men and began to cross the border. I had passed my first test with flying colours but I was still terrified.

So our story had changed. Muskeen was not with me: instead I was still a deaf mute called Shameem, but now I was off to a wedding. Bloody ridiculous, I thought, but what could I do? I couldn't bail out at this point because the Taliban border soldiers, who were armed with semi-automatics and Kalashnikovs, would probably flog me or worse.

So there I was, Yvonne Ridley, walking across an invisible line between two countries filled with a sense of dread and with tons of adrenaline pumping through my system. I really wanted to shout out and try to run back towards Pasha but, dressed as an Afghan woman, I was trapped in a world of silence and opening my mouth would cost me my life.

The area was bustling with lots of fruit stalls interspersed with lockups that sold motor oils and second-hand car accessories. A line of yellow and white cabs waited for new passengers and ragged children were offering all sorts of services from shoeshine to car cleaning to help fill their hungry bellies.

There were a few refugees but there appeared to be more people arriving that day than leaving, and they were nearly all strong, determined young men who strode purposefully into Torkham wanting to fight for the Taliban. I wondered where they had come from and whether there were any European Muslim volunteers among them who were answering the Taliban call for jihad, or holy war.

I walked obediently behind my two guides, but it was so difficult walking in the burka. My vision was blurred and I couldn't see anything in front of me. I was scared that I would trip up or do something out of character and be caught.

The little girl squeezed my hand and once again I thought about the children. I didn't need or want the responsibility of having to watch out for the woman and her two children. The stakes were now much higher and I was angry that I had been compromised like this. I couldn't understand why Muskeen had bottled out because he seemed so keen and enthusiastic about the idea.

He had come up with my name and the plan to go into Afghanistan as a couple. He had even suggested we take along his 11-year-old daughter but I had rejected the idea. I didn't want that responsibility and now here I was with two kids and their mother.

The guides negotiated a deal and we all climbed into the taxi to head for Jalalabad. The road, for want of a better description, was potholed and without tarmac and, sitting in the back, we were constantly thrown around. My head kept banging off a handle above the window and it really hurt.

The taxi driver moaned about something and stopped his car. He looked at the rear wheel and shouted, and the two men also jumped out. One of the rear tyres was punctured and so they set about fixing it. Ten minutes later, we were on the road again and I was impressed at how quickly they had changed the wheel. Suddenly, there was a loud bang and the car swerved on the dirt-track road, which was littered with rubble. We had another puncture. How unlucky is that?

As they changed the wheel I wondered just how many spares the driver was carrying. I was certainly impressed with the fact that he was able to deal with two punctures without too much hassle. Still, two punctures in five minutes did not bode well. Maybe it was Fate trying to intervene in my journey.

The dramatic backdrop of the Hindu Kush mountains gave way to flat planes, stretching out before us, where spindly-looking corn and sugar-cane crops grew.

There was no sign of the Scud missile launchers that were supposed to be positioned towards Pakistan. In fact there was no sign of any military activity, which seemed strange for a country that was about to come under attack from one of the most sophisticated war machines in the world. I saw one MLRS (or multilaunch rocket system) just after we had left the border.

As the taxi jumped, lurched and trundled over the 50-kilometre (31-mile) journey to Jalalabad, I began to feel more relaxed and I began to nod off. I felt really exhausted, possibly because of all the tension and adrenaline. I awoke very suddenly on the outskirts of Jalalabad after banging my head on the handgrip. I panicked for half a second, thinking the knock had damaged my vision, and then I remembered I was wearing the burka.

Ninety minutes earlier my heart had been pounding as I walked across the border and past Taliban soldiers. I had that same feeling again as we arrived in Jalalabad, because every other man seemed to be a Talib and they were all armed and looked very dangerous.

Life looked strangely normal in the bustling town. We stepped out of the taxi and I followed the woman to one corner of the market. She glided gracefully down and balanced herself on the back of her heels while Jan tapped me on the shoulder and hissed, 'Sit!' Ignoring all my Western instincts to snap back, I obeyed the order, but, instead of gliding like my female companion, I went butt first and hit the ground like a sack of potatoes.

Thankfully, this ungainly performance did not attract any attention at all and I thought to myself: What do you have to do to get noticed around here? I was gaining in confidence by the minute because I truly was invisible. From my lowly position I began to observe market life.

There was stall after stall of pomegranates, fat apples and other ripe fruit. I'm not a big fruit eater, much to the annoyance of Mum, but it all looked very good. I bet there's no GM food here and I bet it's all organically grown, I thought to myself. I bet Mullah Omar would ban GM food and anyone caught selling or eating it would be stoned! I wanted to giggle but then I remembered where I was and how so much as a snigger could cost me my life.

My calf muscles were beginning to ache and I felt wobbly. I looked around at my female companion and she looked completely composed and motionless. I should have joined Pilates classes – you know, that form of exercise that improves flexibility – with my friend Daphne Romney. Daffers, as she is known by her close friends, is a top employment and libel lawyer in London who pays for regular punishing workouts at the hands of man I only know as 'Mike the trainer'.

I get exhausted just listening to what she's done. I've tried the keep-fit lark before but I get so bored with all that repetitive exercise and treadmills that take you nowhere. Anyway, I bet Daffers could hang round Jalalabad market all day squatting on her heels. I was thankful when I saw my two guides approaching with various bits of produce and rice they had bought.

They then walked straight past, completely ignoring me. There wasn't a bloody thing I could do but just continue to squat and keep my mouth shut. I followed them in the direction of a meat stall, which was swarming with flies. There was only one joint – it looked like lamb – hanging from a wooden frame. I could barely see through the flaming burka to see what was on the counter, but it looked like minced meat of some sort.

I noticed there were very few women around, but those who dared go out wore burkas. Men lounged around sipping coffee and heavily sugared green tea at one corner of the market while others sipped Coke. The majority chewed a green tobacco-like substance which was spat out indiscriminately at regular intervals accompanied by disgusting throaty sounds.

I think it was a product from the plant *khat*, which has some sort of hallucinatory effect. I remember because we did a story when I worked for *Wales on Sunday* about a grocer's shop in Cardiff's Yemeni community which sold *khat* and when the supplier arrived on Wednesdays there was always a huge queue. I hasten to add that at the moment it is perfectly legal to get high chewing the leaves of this plant.

From my little perch by the roadside I watched a typical market, even though I felt completely abandoned. The heat was stifling and I continued to gasp for air while my guides took a leisurely stroll around the market, chewing the fat with old friends and bartering with stallholders.

Eventually they returned and I had a face like thunder, except that no one noticed because, of course, I was hidden by my burka. We took another taxi ride through the town on a three-wheeled, colourfully painted type of motorised rickshaw.

For some strange reason the town appeared to be full of pharmacies and motor accessory shops. Clothes shops were nonexistent. I found out later that Mullah Omar had decreed that women were forbidden from buying new clothes because of the impending jihad. Daffers, who is a complete 'clothesaholic', couldn't survive in a regime like this. In fact she'd take herself out to a field and stone herself!

Afterwards, our party took one of the yellow and white taxis into the countryside four miles east of Jalalabad. The driver stopped his car in the middle of nowhere and we got out. I'm only *pretending* to be a deaf mute, I wanted to scream. Will someone *please* tell me what's going on? But two women were walking past and I could not draw any attention to myself.

As I was about to discover, we were going to visit a village called Kama. It is a tiny little place and it looked very insignificant.

But it was going to have a huge, haunting impact on my life.

6

INTO THE HANDS OF THE TALIBAN

The fields were green and fresh in Afghanistan and the corn and sugar cane looked quite plump and healthy, much healthier than the crops I saw near the border at Torkham. We walked single file over a winding, narrow path through one of the fields. I was acting as tail-end Charley and I could hardly see where I was going because of the lace grille on my burka. I really had to crick my neck down to follow the path and make sure I didn't tumble or fall over any obstacles.

I also knew that somewhere round this region was one of Osama bin Laden's base camps, but I was too busy trying to concentrate on following the path to look around. Such behaviour would have been seen as suspicious, anyway.

For all I knew the world's most wanted man could have been a few miles away. Actually he could have been a few *feet* away and I wouldn't have noticed him.

We reached a tiny footbridge, which gently arched over a stream. Suddenly, some mud-caked brick walls loomed from nowhere to reveal Kama, a typical Afghan village.

A woman came rushing out of the village entrance to hug and kiss everyone, including me, although how she knew we were arriving at that moment is beyond me. I have no idea who she thought I was but I found myself being greeted like a long-lost relative. The two girls went off to join the swarms of other children who were playing in a large courtyard.

There was a reedlike overhang adjoining one of the courtyard walls and it gave shelter to the cooking area. On another side was a hand-cranked water pump, and some battered pots and pans were hanging out to dry.

My female companion pulled my arm and we went into a large room. It had the usual Afghan rug surrounded by lots of cushions and mattresses. She motioned to a mattress. I was so shattered I lifted up the burka and curled up on one of the mattresses to go to sleep. For someone who hates sleeping, it may seem odd that I seemed to be fighting off tiredness. Maybe it was down to nervous exhaustion, the heat, the long walk or the fact that I hadn't really had a good night's sleep for two days.

Outside, there was great excitement as relatives and friends greeted each other and no doubt gossiped. I managed to drift off to sleep and about an hour later there was a young man kneeling by me urging me to wake up. I went cold with fear because he was speaking to me in English.

I slipped the burka back over my face and sat up, still maintaining a silence. 'It's OK, it's OK,' he reassured me. 'I know who you are. Jan told me and I think you are a great woman to come here. Take off your burka and let us talk.'

Nevertheless, I maintained my silence, trying to work out how he knew who and what I was, when Jan walked in and said, 'I have told them and it is safe for you to talk here.'

Shocked and disorientated because my cover as a deaf mute had been blown, I lifted off the burka, pulled on a headscarf and scowled at Jan.

'Please don't be unhappy. You are quite safe and your visit will remain secret,' he said in a kind voice. Jan was a tall, willowy man, around 25, whose good looks were masked by a scraggy bush of a beard.

His uncle, my other guide, then strode into the room. I did not like him at all and have no logical reason for this instant dislike, because we could not communicate. He had a long, thin face and an unkempt beard and I don't think I ever saw him smile once. He was about ten years older than Jan.

'Tell me, why do you come here?' asked the young man, who was in his early twenties. 'You know this is very dangerous for you.'

For the first time in about eight hours I was able to talk without being guarded. It was wonderful to be able to say, 'I am a British journalist and I want to do a story about people like you who are living in Afghanistan. I want to know your hopes and fears, your ambitions and what do you think about what happened on September the eleventh and talk about American reprisals.'

He told me he wanted to train as a doctor but that the schools in the district had been closed, and so it was impossible for him to follow his ambitions. I sympathised with him, and then he said everyone was really shocked about the 11 September 'mishap'. I don't know why it is but even in Pakistan the terrorist strike was constantly referred to as the 'mishap'.

Just then I looked up and around thirty to forty people had gathered, silently, in the room. The young man spoke to them and repeated what I had said. A little girl knelt by me and began fanning me heavily with a fan fashioned from reed.

I asked if I could take a picture and produced my camera. 'Taliban do not allow pictures to be taken,' said the young man sternly. So I put the camera back down. I asked what else the Taliban did not like and a woman of about 25 spoke up and talked about being denied an education.

Translating her story, the English-speaker said, 'She was training to become a doctor when education was suddenly withdrawn from the women.'

Her strong features were masked by hardship and sadness. There is no place for career women in Afghanistan; it's as though they didn't exist. She seemed grateful that I acknowledged her intelligence and I got the distinct impression of solidarity between the two of us – two women from greatly different worlds, cultures and backgrounds.

I wondered how I would cope under such an existence. Of course, you don't cope: you exist. I was touched by the people of Kama because they were so kind and generous in heart and spirit. It was quite obvious to me that they feared little and, although they were praying for a peaceful outcome, they were still prepared to fight to preserve their independence.

Although burka-clad Afghan women give the impression of servility, the women from Kama were strong, spirited and resilient. One woman, who had the most amazing almond-shaped, hazel eyes and magnificent cheekbones, gently mocked me when she asked if I had any children and I said 'one'.

Putting her hands on a fine pair of child-bearing hips she mocked: 'Only one? Ha! You British and American women can only produce one or two children but I can have fifteen, and when you run out of your boy soldiers to send to war we will have many replacements. Our children are born with guns in their hands. They are fighters and will die fighting. It is part of our life and our struggle. If I have to fight I will and so will she,' she said, pointing her long, bony fingers at an old woman whose tiny, crumpled frame and toothless smile radiated great wisdom.

I was told she was a hundred years old and that she had seen many wars. She shouted something at me and everyone laughed. She had said of course she would fight the American soldiers and said no one could conquer the Afghan people. I was then reminded of a famous saying, which goes, 'Anyone can rent an Afghani but no one can own one.'

By this time the woman with the hazel eyes had taken centre stage and through the young translator she said, 'We heard about what happened in New York and we are sorry so many innocent people died. I hope the Americans think twice before trying to bomb us but whatever happens we are not afraid.'

I am sure she, like the others, was quite genuine in her sentiments, but I doubt that they could really comprehend the full scale of the disaster that unfolded before every television viewer in the world. Of course, TV is banned in Afghanistan and news in these forgotten parts is usually by word of mouth or radio.

As a result, not many would have seen the horrific images that have left many of us emotionally scarred for life.

Most Afghan people lucky enough to have a roof over their heads can imagine a single-storey building because there are lots of those in the country, but, when you ask them to try to think in terms of a hundred storeys upwards, their imagination is challenged.

Most of the adult men had drifted off but the young translator continued to talk and he admitted sadly, 'There is nothing for me here and we are all very poor. It is difficult to escape from this poverty and follow my ambitions. Very few of us can afford to have ambitions.'

His last line stung me. Everyone needs an ambition, something to drive them along. Why can't the Taliban ease off and let these people breathe? Perhaps the movement started off with the best of intentions, but it had somehow lost its way.

The women had truly striking features and I suddenly realised that, until this moment, I did not know what Afghan women looked like and what lay beneath the burka. I think they were as fascinated with me as I was with them. When I removed the burka I noticed black stains from some of the hair dye that had not been as effective as it might have been under better conditions. The baking heat, the closeness of the burka and my sweat had forced the colour to run from my hair, which felt and looked like straw. Thankfully, my scarf covered up most of that.

The woman who saw herself as an invincible baby machine yanked me to my feet and pulled me outside to have some food. Their generosity is overwhelming and, although they have little, what little they have they wanted me to share.

I had missed the rice, stew and bread, which was eaten with skilful fingers, so she threw me a succulent corn on the cob and roared with laughter because I squealed and dropped it, it was so hot. Once again she made a mocking gesture and told the onlookers that women from the West were soft. I could tell that by her gestures.

She then picked up the cob from the dusty ground and pulled out a rag and proceeded to clean the cob before handing it back to me. I knew that refusal to eat a second time would offend the hospitality so I happily munched on the corn, served with butter.

After that I was given a piece of sugar cane to chew, which was quite refreshing. I watched others eating it, too, and was relieved when they spat out the dry pulp, which I was attempting to swallow. I felt very humbled by their generosity and kindness.

A girl aged about twelve began to crank out some water from the pump in the barren yard to wash all of the battered, metal plates and pans. I noticed a neighbour from an adjoining home peering over the wall, probably to see what all the noise was about. There was a lot of loud banter, giggling and laughter – all the sort of things the Taliban don't like. I was fearful when I saw her and when she saw me she couldn't stop staring and I felt a shiver go down my spine.

Just then one of the young men came out into the yard with my camera and began taking pictures – another big no-no. Jan asked if I still wanted to stay overnight and I said that we should really go.

I would have liked to stay and I was enjoying the freedom of not wearing that bloody stifling garment, but my instincts were telling me to get the hell out of there. I still hadn't been able to remonstrate with my guides and could not wait to get them on their own to give them a piece of my mind!

The six of us set off from the village through a three-foot-high exit, which I assumed must be some sort of escape route for occasions when you might want to avoid the neighbours or unwelcome visitors. We headed back for the dirt track to wait for the taxi. It came along about forty minutes later. I don't know how the driver knew we would be standing there, unless he just happened to be driving by. Jan and his uncle crossed the road to speak to someone they knew, but not before I had been tapped on the shoulder and told, 'Sit!'

Going down to the ground was no easier this time, and once again I crashed unceremoniously bottom first. While I was sitting there I noticed a big brown creature weaving in and out of the cornfield on the opposite side of the road. I'm not sure what it was but it looked like some sort of otter to me. It was about the size of a cat with a fat, long, trailing tale.

I was relieved to get in the taxi and couldn't wait to get over into Pakistan. I was cutting my visit short because I felt nervous about what had happened in the village although I had better material than I expected. The original idea was for Muskeen to be my eyes and ears in Jalalabad and after two days we would return to Pakistan and he would tell Pasha everything he heard and saw and Pasha would tell me. I would add in the colour I saw and then we would be able to present a good, all-round feature.

I wonder whether readers really appreciate the work that is done behind the scenes to bring fresh news to their breakfast tables. Quite often the story behind the story is far more entertaining than the one that gets into the paper.

The journey on that road was hellish as we were being thrown around in the car. The younger of the two girls started crying and the other one had nodded off, although how she managed to sleep I don't know.

I wanted to go to the toilet and wished I had asked back at the village.

I tried to memorise each image I saw as we headed to Torkham, because I was convinced I would never be coming back to this country again. Yes, the people were nice – in fact they were bloody lovely – but the country itself did nothing for me.

When we finally arrived in Torkham, the sun had gone down. I'm not sure what the time was because I had left my watch in the hotel safe. I had taken nothing of value with me, no money, no earrings, no jewellery and certainly not my passport. The last thing I wanted was to get kidnapped by some feuding tribal gang who might steal my passport or use me as some sort of bargaining chip.

If the Taliban capture me, I told myself, I will most likely be executed but, then again, if they want to hear my story first I can tell them there is a copy of my passport on the bloody visa application at the Islamabad embassy. It was an irrelevant argument, anyway, because there we were in Torkham, a stone's throw away from the border.

Suddenly Jan directed me to a side of the road, tapped me on the shoulder and ordered in a hushed tone, 'Sit!' I complied, smug in the knowledge that that bastard was going to get such a mouthful once I got over the border. I might even start a burn-the-burka campaign just as women had burned their bras in the sixties.

I squatted with my female companion and her two little girls. We were hunched and balancing on our toes while resting our bottoms on our heels, four little maids in a row. After half an hour the two guides came back, stony-faced and silent. We got up and some words were said to the woman. Our party turned around and headed for a saloon-type bar that did not serve alcohol.

There were loads of people milling around, looking and sounding agitated, but I could not make out what was going on. I was concentrating hard, trying to focus from behind my veiled eyes in the pitch black. The six of us entered a carpeted room. There were no windows, no fan and no ventilation.

That was it! I wrenched up my burka and said to Jan, 'Right, you'd better tell me what's going on. This is my bloody operation, my job, I am directing you two and when I tell you to bloody jump you ask me how high. If you want to see a single rupee from me you'd better start showing me some respect. Now tell him,' I said waving my finger at the pair of them.

Jan relayed the conversation on. I can tell he did so faithfully, because the other bloke was stony-faced and kept giving me black, thunderous looks. He then said something back and there seemed to be a heated exchange.

Jan turned round and said, 'You must lower your voice or people will suspect you. We have a problem. Pakistan has closed the border and we don't know when it will open again. Even though we have travel papers we cannot get through, so we will have to use an alternative route. We will take one of the smugglers' routes out tomorrow and we will be in Pakistan by the afternoon. In the meantime, we have hired this hotel room.'

I was shaking with rage and feared both for my safety and for that of everyone else. Quaking, I muttered, 'Why am I just hearing about this now? Why did you not raise the alarm sooner. I do not accept this. We have to split up and go different ways because it's obvious to me that if the Taliban aren't looking for us yet they will be by the morning. Someone in the village will have betrayed us.'

Jan looked concerned because he could see I was scared. 'No, don't worry. No one from the village will betray us. We have to stick together. You cannot leave on your own because women do not wander round at this time of night alone, or at any other time.'

My reply was swift: 'These are stressful times and any one person in that village might tell the Taliban, to ingratiate themselves with the regime. If they are looking for us they will be looking for two men, two women and two children. What I suggest we do is split up and leave the family. You and I can head off together. We will all be safer that way.'

He then turned to the guide and had another conversation with him. There was another heated exchange and then the two left the room. I couldn't believe it. They were gone for more than an hour and there was nothing I could do. Despite everything I had said about directing this operation, they had just naffed off and totally ignored me. I sat cross-legged in the corner, with the burka lifted into a cowl position on my head.

I looked at the woman and the two children. I guessed that she was probably no older than thirty at a push, but the hard life of an Afghan woman had taken its toll on her face. She was a good-looking woman, though, and she had the kindest smile, one that radiated warmth and understanding. God knows what she was doing with the plonker, but then again they say love is blind – look at the cock-ups *I've* made in my life!

About an hour later the heroes returned with some food. I declined to eat any and remembered I needed to go to the toilet. I hadn't been all day. I asked Jan where they were and he directed me outside and across a road and pointed in the inky blackness. I couldn't see a thing, and then I realised he expected me to climb down a ravine in the darkness to have a pee.

Quite how I got the strength I don't know, but I maintained total bladder control and refused to go. There are snakes and scorpions in Afghanistan, and other poisonous things, and I wasn't going to take my chances.

I marched back and Jan whispered for me to slow down and get behind him. I kept forgetting I was supposed to be an Afghan. I huddled in a corner and was bitten several times by mosquitoes on my hands, the only bit of skin exposed. The night passed so slowly. I tried to sleep but a sickening fear kept me awake. I wondered what everyone at work would be doing and whether anyone was that concerned about my little sojourn into Afghanistan. My last text message was from Keith Perry and it had read: JIM SAYS BE CAREFUL AS WE DON'T WANT TO LOSE YOU! LUV KEITH.

Pasha had my phone and I wondered whether my mother had called yet or even whether she had realised things were going pear-shaped over here. Of course I would have to tell Joyce where I had been and what I was up to because she reads the paper every Sunday and she would soon find out. She'll probably just roll her eyes heavenwards, I thought, and be thankful she didn't know I was in until I was out. Then she'll say to me, 'You've got that bairn to think about. What's going to happen to her if something happens to you? Your dad and I are too old to look after Daisy.'

I had actually thought about it earlier this year and had taken out a special insurance to ensure that Daisy's private education will continue until she reaches eighteen. I'm not a morose person, but I am practical.

My thoughts then drifted towards the next week and I thought I would try to go to Kandahar, but I would not be taking the two guides I was using for this trip. They were undisciplined and downright bloody rude. They'd obviously never heard of the saying, 'Don't bite the hand that feeds you.'

Maybe Muskeen would agree to go this time or Pasha would have to find me somebody else. If it didn't look likely then I supposed that I could follow the original plan and try to get into one of the terrorist training camps in Kashmir.

Of course, the war could have started and by then there would be loads of copy to write. There were all sorts of ideas raging around in my head and I sighed and huffed and puffed in this sweaty room. I don't know how they could have called it a hotel because there was no room service, no bathroom and no toilet facilities.

At around 5 a.m. our party stirred and we went outside towards another taxi. We then drove off towards the Hindu Kush mountain range. There were no roads, just well-worn routes, and the driver went as far as he could in his saloon car. We got out and a stony-covered mountain pass lay ahead.

The two guides went off to pray and I motioned to the woman that I needed to go to the toilet. I hadn't been for 24 hours and I was fit to burst. She pointed over to some rocks and I set about the complicated procedure of trying to undo garments and trousers and knickers while still wearing the burka.

Relief was swift and I started to relax and wind down a bit more. I looked up at the sky and saw a shooting star, so made a wish. It was an easy wish: 'Get me out of here!' And then I watched the star, waiting for it to begin to vaporise, but it didn't. I lifted up my burka and pushed it back over my forehead and watched it closely.

Oh, my God! I thought to myself. It's a bloody satellite capturing a snapshot of life down here and now there'll be an image of me having a pee! Some of these satellites can create an image to one metre! Mind you, I was wearing my burka, so I could be anybody. I wondered whether it was a military satellite or a commercial one. But it didn't matter: it was definitely a satellite of some sort and not a star.

I pulled the burka back over my face, stood up and then turned around to walk towards the woman – and went flat on my face. I'd been too busy watching the satellite that I had forgotten to fasten my trousers and they had dropped to my ankles.

Having hoisted myself back up, I tied my trousers. When I crossed over the road the woman had her burka lifted above her face and she was laughing. It was silent laughter, but it was laughter all the same, and, although I'd made a complete prat of myself, I was glad I was able to bring laughter to her face.

A few minutes later my eyes were welling up in tears. We started to climb up the narrow pass and the hard plastic shoes I was wearing began to cut angrily into my skin like jagged teeth. A blister, which had developed nicely on my right heel, burst and the pain was searing.

I'm sure I was not alone in suffering from the climb, but everyone using the route was silent and uncomplaining. There must be around four hundred illegal routes through Pakistan's porous 1,400-mile-long border.

As the sun emerged I noticed that the magnificent slopes of the Hindu Kush mountains were teaming with fit, agile tribesmen who come and go through the border with the greatest of ease. With the grace of gazelles they climbed almost sheer slopes, looking down on the rest of us mere mortals with disdain.

When we reached Daur Baba, there were quite a few men milling around and very few women. Camels and trains of donkeys lined up to carry smuggled goods, chattels and people over the border. I looked out for refugees but could see only a handful. I wondered what had happened to the tens of thousands who had turned up at Torkham some days earlier. I think quite a few may have gone south towards Quetta.

Once again, Jan tapped me on the shoulder and I went down to squat. He smiled one of his kind smiles and I could almost forgive him for the previous day. He whispered to me, 'Yvonne, you are now safe. You can lift your burka, although try to keep your face covered. If you want to take any pictures you can. I was so sorry for you last night. You were suffering so much from the heat but it is nearly all over. We are less than twenty minutes from the Pakistan border and you will ride over on a donkey.'

I gave a huge sigh of relief because I don't think I could have taken another step in those shoes that I had been given the day before. I remained squatting and gently lifted up my burka and enjoyed a cooling breeze on my face.

The woman was sitting there with her younger daughter and I motioned to take her picture, and she agreed. I got a beautiful portrait shot and then I turned around and took several landscape shots, capturing this chaotic scene of traders, smugglers, refugees and tribesmen swarming around the hills at Daur Baba.

Jan led me to the donkey and I was taken to a platform and climbed on to the animal. One of my trouser legs rode up and I revealed an ankle, which was thankfully covered by my dad's socks. I was busy rearranging my clothes and burka when the damned donkey shot forward as if to bolt.

The English Northern expression 'Flaming Nora!' spilled involuntarily from my mouth as I bellowed my first public words in two days. It was not Pushtu and several people looked in my direction although clearly did not understand that I had just cursed in English. What had attracted their attention was a noisy woman in a burka. Afghan women are not meant to be noisy. They are meant to be servile and quiet.

Most people had returned to what had been occupying their minds before I had cried out, and, as I tried to regain some composure, I leaned forward to grab the rein. The movement caused my camera to move into full view and a Taliban soldier shouted out at me and gestured for me to get off the donkey.

I will never forget the look on the face of the soldier. Not because he was about to arrest me and probably kill me but because he had the most amazing emerald-green eyes I have ever seen. Bizarre as it may seem, I was totally captivated by his breathtaking features, albeit momentarily.

He wrenched me off the donkey and motioned for me to remove the camera. I quickly obeyed and he grabbed it from me, then shouted something at the donkey's owner, who pointed in the direction of Jan's uncle. He marched over to him and asked him some questions and hit him heavily across the face with the back of his hand, causing his nose to bleed.

Jan went to his uncle's defence and tried to reason with the Talib, who was shouting and screaming. Within seconds a crowd of up to two hundred men had gathered around and in their eagerness to find out what was going on I was pushed further and further back. I deliberated for a few minutes and thought to myself: I can turn around and walk towards the border because they are more interested in the guides. I will be able to tag along with others, and because I'm wearing the burka, I'm still invisible.

It was a hard call to make and in the end I couldn't leave the two guides behind. I watched as the wife calmly disappeared with the younger daughter and I forced my way back into the crowd and asked the soldier for my camera back.

The soldier with the green eyes looked incredulous. He had obviously forgotten about me and here I was speaking to him in a strange tongue. By this time more Taliban men were at the scene and they gasped, as they could see that I was a Western woman. The crowd began to jostle me and a flame-haired Talib grabbed me and the camera and took me to a car.

7

CAPTIVITY

As the car drove away from the Pakistan border I became numb with fear and my whole body seemed to switch off. Maybe it was a defence mechanism, but I remained totally calm on the outside. Inside, the adrenaline was shooting round my system and I could hear my heart thumping as I tried to work out the best course of action.

My train of thought was shattered by semiautomatic gunfire, which ripped through the air. Our car had become part of a convoy and was being led by a lorry load of young soldiers screaming triumphantly, 'Amreeka spy, Amreeka spy!' Oh, great, I thought, they think I'm a bloody American. Well I needed that like I needed a hole in the head.

Just then I felt a very sharp nip on my arm. It was the Afghan guide. He was waving and crossing his hands and putting his hand to his mouth. I got the message instantly and if he had taken any notice of me from the beginning he would have known what the plan was in the event of our arrest: 'We are all on a need-to-know basis and I don't need to know your names,' I had told them through Pasha. 'The less I know about you the better, in the unlikely event we are caught.'

There was more gunfire and the excited rabble then began chanting that phrase so favoured by young Muslims during Peshawar demonstrations: 'Osama *zindabad*, Osama *zindabad*!' they crowed, which means long life to

Mr bin Laden. What about long life to Yvonne Ridley? No bloody chance.

The car stopped and Jan was removed. I didn't think I would ever see him again. Another man got in the car and sat next to me. I don't think he was a Taliban soldier and he wasn't wearing one of those heavy turbans – which, by the way, I think we might see reflected on the fashion catwalks of Europe for 2002.

So, fashion tip aside, I had the Afghan guide on one side and this oily creature on the other. The Afghan continued to nip me hard and twist my skin. I had already got the message and if he continued I swore I'd throttle him if it was the last thing I did.

The car stopped again and Jan was returned to the vehicle. He looked OK. It was a pleasant surprise that he was back in our company. Sadly, his return meant that I was squeezed next to this other man, who had begun to touch me. At first I thought it was an accident, but then I realised he was trying to grope me. I hoped he would stop although at that moment I thought it was the least of my problems.

The Afghan squeezed and nipped my skin hard, and then I snapped. I had to get a message through that I would keep my mouth shut. So I bellowed, 'Does anyone in this car understand English?' Of course there was silence, so I continued: 'I don't know what the hell is going on. I don't know who these two men are but I am a British subject and if I don't get my camera back there will be serious trouble.'

At least Jan would be able to tell the Afghan so he would stop hurting me. The creep on my right pulled at my burka and off it came, revealing black-blonde, matted, strawlike hair. I had no make-up on. My complexion is normally a milky white with splodges of freckles and I have blue eyes.

The creep gave me a comb and I tried to comb my hair, which had been flattened and ruined from two days underneath that burka. At least it was off now, which was a relief. Even Pollyanna would have approved of that positive note in these critical circumstances.

I was wearing some pale-orange trousers and a matching orange, floral dress with three big flowers stuck on the front. The waistline dipped in modestly, then the skirt sprang out like a lampshade. It was a horrendous outfit and I looked like Bette Davis in *Whatever Happened to Baby Jane?*.

The front-seat passenger with the flame hair kept looking round at me and at first he seemed to be eyeing me up and down. Christ, I am probably going to be raped or gang-raped, I thought.

Suddenly the driver was ordered to stop and I was removed from the car by the Talib, who placed me on some high ground. He then disappeared and within minutes another crowd had gathered around and all I could see was a mass of angry and curious faces.

They were shouting and screaming and jabbering in an excited fashion. Looking back I suppose I was a bit of light entertainment that had been brought into their mundane existence. At that time, though, I had gone cold with fear. And my mouth had gone as dry as a carpet.

I looked down and I saw blood-red nail polish staring up at me. My shoes had gone and so had my socks, although I don't remember when or how. I hoped no one would notice my infidel-coloured toes because I knew varnish was on the banned list.

I looked back at the crowd and said to myself: This is it. It's the end. I am going to be stoned to death. Please, God, let the first stone knock me unconscious and make me strong enough so I don't plead for my life.

I wondered how much pain I could take and prayed that whatever happened I would die quickly. I then pondered what would happen to my body, and whether it would be sent home. I wondered whether my parents would have to identify it or whether Daisy would ever be told how I died. Would *anyone* be told? I asked myself.

The crowd moved in closer and I wanted to close my eyes but I felt maybe I could stare them out or perhaps someone might connect with me and pity me and try to stop the stoning. I looked at the ground and there was enough ammunition to keep the *intifada* (the Palestinian uprising against Israel in the West Bank and Gaza Strip) going for another decade.

Just then I caught the Taliban soldier in the corner of my eye flagging down a passing car. A woman in a burka was asked to get out and he pointed in my direction. The two began walking towards me but by this time the crowd were chanting. I thought chanting was banned.

The woman spun me around and started to search me in a very rough manner. I've never been so relieved in my life. What joy! I said to myself. They think I've got a weapon or something secret on me. And then my relief turned to anger.

I swung around at the crowd and went to lift up my dress in defiance as if to say: Go on, then, take a look. Not even a stick of dynamite. It was a gesture that provoked outrage, shock and anger and earned me a well-deserved slap across my face.

The vulgar act caused the crowd of men to gasp and then turn in the other direction and run. It was a bizarre sight and made me remember the *Carry On Up the Khyber* film, in which kilted soldiers lift their skirts up to frighten off the natives. It was highly inappropriate behaviour and consequently the woman in the burka lifted her arms and hit me. I don't know who was more in shock, she or I – or even the flame-haired soldier.

Our convoy continued on the hellish journey back to Jalalabad and the creep continued to grope me. My patience finally snapped and I shouted, 'Stop it!' I then dug him sharply in the ribs and he yelped. The front-seat passenger witnessed half of what had happened and ordered the driver to stop the car.

A heated exchange followed between the passenger and the creep and within thirty seconds he had been ejected from the car. Our journey continued along with the gunfire and the chanting, which was very unnerving.

As we reached Jalalabad, I was paraded around every street-corner checkpoint and shown off like some kind of trophy. I wound my window down and asked if anyone spoke English and the response was no. A little boy, probably Daisy's age, grimaced and stared at me through the window.

He had a mop of curly, wild hair and brown eyes with a pale, olive skin. He looked really cute and I smiled at him. He cocked his head sideways and, lifting a dirty little finger, he drew it across his neck. Charming! I've never really liked little boys and this one was a complete stinker.

As we pulled away for the next checkpoint the driver gave a throaty cough and spat out the heavily chewed lump of *ghat* he'd had in his mouth. Wrapped in his phlegm, the whole pile landed on my face and, as it slid down, I retched before using the burka to wipe myself.

We stopped at another checkpoint and a man gave me some paper and a pen and I quickly scribbled Jim Murray's work telephone number on it and begged the man to ring. He couldn't speak a word of English and I think what he was after was my signature. It was probably going to be the last time I put pen to paper, I thought to myself.

The shock was starting to wear off and the full horror of what lay in store started to dawn on me. I think my eyes became quite moist and this man put his arm through the car door and gripped my wrist in a firm but harmless way. He kept saying 'OK' and I think he was trying to reassure me. I smiled at him and he smiled back.

Looking back, I realise that it must have been quite a memorable moment for the men of Jalalabad, who saw only the faces of their mothers, wives or sisters. There, sitting in the back of this car, was a blonde-haired, blue-eyed woman from the West who was not wearing a burka. If I had still been undercover, no one would have bothered me.

The car pulled off and we eventually headed through the gates of the Taliban intelligence headquarters. The three of us and the little girl were taken into a plain, but clean, air conditioned room with bathroom facilities and left on our own while the door was locked. I motioned to Jan to say nothing in case it was bugged. The Afghan had finally got the message: I was not going to say or do anything to betray them.

About half an hour later we were ushered out and into another room with a single, hospital-style bed. I gestured to the jailer that I couldn't be left in a room with two strange men whom I didn't know. It was a situation that was not allowed in the Taliban regime and I tried to use it to my advantage. It worked and I was put back in the original room on my own.

My personal jailer, who could not speak a word of English, motioned to me that he was going to lock the door from the outside and that if I wanted anything I would have to knock. Like many Taliban soldiers, he was quite striking to look at and had a magnificent, wild main of thick curly hair under his bronze-coloured turban, which was wrapped around an extravagantly covered tribal cap. The cap told me that he came from the Kondoz region in the northeast, and is supposed to contain more than two thousand different colours.

I sat down on one of the red mattresses and tried to assess my situation and my chances of survival, and I have to say that things did not look that good. I wondered what the time was and thought Jim would be at the newsdesk now waiting for my call.

I felt really sick and scared and wondered whether the world would ever find out that I was being held by the Taliban. I wondered what had happened to my camera and remembered that a commission from *Nikon Owner*, the magazine of the Nikon Owners' Club International, had just gone down the tubes.

It is funny how trivia seems to come to the surface in really serious and heavy situations. I was worrying about what was on the film and wondered whether they could identify any of the villagers from Kama. All sorts of crazy thoughts were racing through my mind, and I realised I still had my hands wrapped round the burka.

Just then I heard what was to become a familiar sound: the lock rattling and the key turning. It was the director of intelligence, a cool, elegant man whose face betrayed no emotion of any kind. His eyes were cold and my imagination began to run riot. I wondered whether he carried out his own torture or was one of those who would cast the first stone.

There was something very enigmatic about him. He asked me to write down some personal details and I informed him that I was a British journalist. He remained unimpressed and I got the feeling if I said I was a messenger sent by the Queen of England he would still have hung on to his deadpan expression.

After he left I felt quite pleased with myself because I had managed to hang on to his pen. All I needed was some paper or other writing material and I would be back in business as a journalist.

It was Friday afternoon, 28 September, a day that will live with me for the rest of my life, and I don't think many of my family, friends or colleagues will forget it, either. I wondered when Jim would sound the alarm and did not envy him the task of breaking the news to my mum and dad. He was after all the bloke, in Mum's eyes, who had sent her baby daughter off to Islamabad. In many ways I was in the best place and at least my sense of humour was intact.

I looked around the room, which had an air-conditioning unit, to see what I could find. I found a coffee-table book, which had been given to someone as a farewell gift because it had loads of signatures inside from well-wishers. I got the feeling it had belonged – or had even perhaps been presented – to someone in Britain or America who was making a new life out in Afghanistan. It was called *Caravans to Tatary* and was written by a French couple called Roland and Sabria Michaud.

The book was first published in 1978 and was about the Michauds themselves, who had obviously travelled across Afghanistan taking some stunning pictures and dramatic snapshots of Afghan life. I wondered about the original owner of the book and pondered on why it had been left behind. Whatever the reason, I was glad because it kept me occupied me for a short while.

If I didn't keep active my mind would start to drift towards Taliban punishments, including stoning and beheading. Anyone who has watched Saira Shah's shocking television documentary, *Beneath the Veil*, would know how evil this regime can be.

I think she hid a camera beneath her burka and sneaked into the country to expose the brutality of the Taliban towards women. She secretly filmed some public executions at football pitches. I wondered whether she would film mine.

As I sat there twiddling my thumbs I got a whiff of something really smelly – and realised it was me. I hadn't had a bath for more than two days and I had been wearing a dress and trousers made of nylon, Crimplene and polyester. I was smelly and sweaty, and my hair was plastered to my head.

The jailer, whose name, I was to discover, was Abdullah Mounir, returned with some food and I refused to eat it. I hadn't eaten for about two days but with all the anger, excitement, tension and fear the last thing on my mind was food. Abdullah spoke no English but using my hands I made it clear I would not eat unless I spoke to my mum on the telephone.

The director, who could understand bits of English, returned and asked why I was not eating. He was joined by three other Taliban people and a young man called Hamid, who was to be the translator. I said, arms folded, 'I will not eat anything until I can speak to my mother and I certainly cannot eat your food as a prisoner. I will eat with the Taliban only as their guest.'

They looked at me and I thought: Ridley, where the hell did that pompous twaddle come from? They obviously thought the same, because they walked out and left me with no food and no phone. I looked out of the window, which was covered in mosquito netting, and contemplated my future.

I had no more visitors and went to sleep, or tried to. During the early hours of the morning I heard the door open and the hair on the back of my neck began to prickle, but I did not stir. I was curled in a foetal position and by squinting I could see the outline of a man standing at the door.

The door then closed and everything was pitch black. I was about to let out a sigh of relief when I released the man was in my room. I didn't know whether I should scream, but I don't think a noise would have come out, anyway, because my mouth was like sandpaper.

The man knelt down and watched me, thinking I was asleep. I locked my eyes and felt his presence there for quite a while. He then lay down on the mattress beside me and shook me gently. I sat up and looked at him and then huge tears just rolled silently down my cheeks.

Although my eyes had become accustomed to the darkness I could see only a black outline of a Talib, but he could see me from the moonlight. He raised his arm and I flinched in fear. I pleaded: 'Please God, no.' He stopped, then moved the back of his hand towards my face and gently wiped away the tears. He stood up and said something softly in Pushtu and left.

The next morning Hamid, the civilian translator, came to see me before breakfast and said, 'A man came to me today and he said he was very concerned that your sleep was disturbed.' I told Hamid I had slept very well and did not know what he was talking about. He tried again: 'This man is very concerned that your sleep was disturbed and that you may have been upset.'

I began to realise that whoever had come into my room was in serious trouble and they needed to know whether I was going to complain. I replied, 'No, I was not disturbed last night. Maybe I had a bad dream and if I did it is now gone and forgotten.'

He looked at me strangely and went off to deliver the good news to whoever had come into my room. I certainly did not feel in a position to complain because in their cockeyed world the Taliban would probably rule that it was my fault in the first place.

Secondly, the man could see I was distressed and had had the decency to walk away. I can think of a few Western men who've really got to be bawled and shouted at before they will finally take 'no' for an answer.

Abdullah came in later and pointed to a lock on the inside of the door and through sign language told me I must use this to deter any would-be nocturnal visitors with less than savoury motives.

Once again Hamid, who learned to speak his English in Pakistan, said my decision not to eat was causing consternation. The director arrived, and, although I got the distinct impression he didn't need the services of Hamid, he spoke through him nonetheless. He explained that he could not get me a telephone because the communication systems were so bad that calls could not be made without a satellite telephone.

If they had given me access to a telephone I could have filed my feature about the beautiful people who welcomed me into their homes at Kama village, and given descriptions of life around Jalalabad market. It was a Saturday and it should have been the busiest day of the week for me. I wondered whether news had filtered out yet that I was in the hands of the Taliban.

Two men from Taliban intelligence arrived to interview me. I once again apologised for any problems my capture may have caused them and they seemed to appreciate this gesture. What they could not get their heads around was why someone, even a journalist, would want to go into their country when so many others were trying to get out.

Through Hamid, I tried to explain my business and I told them that about three thousand other media people from newspapers, radio and television were sitting in Pakistan wanting to know what was happening over the border. Clearly they did not understand or even comprehend the media, and once again I asked to use the telephone. This was declined and I exploded.

'If you don't give me the telephone my mother will be distressed. I am sitting in a nice air-conditioned room, in civilised company with access to a flush toilet and a shower and I want to tell her how well you are looking after me.

'She probably doesn't even know I'm here. I will tell her I have a small problem which I am sorting out and she will accept that. Otherwise my newspaper will write big headlines and stories about you. Have you any idea what people in the West think about you people?

They listened impassively as Hamid translated me words. I then added, 'My mother will think I am hanging by my ankles from this ceiling, completely naked, while you are whipping me.' Hamid blushed, hesitated and then spat out the last sentence. They arched their eyebrows and looked at each other and left.

Yes! I thought. I will have a telephone soon. How wrong I was. Even though I was sticking by my hunger strike, food was still brought to me. That night Hamid and Abdullah came in with my food and began eating in front of me. I puffed away on the cigarettes they had given me and drank green tea which was refreshing.

Suddenly a huge explosion ripped through the air and, although I was sitting in a cross legged position, I think I must have leaped about three feet. Hamid sniggered and Abdullah could hardly contain himself with laughter. It was around 5 p.m. and Abdullah grabbed his gun and shouted 'Amreeka, Amreeka' and made the sound of a firing gun. He was gone in an instant and I tried to brace myself because maybe this was the start of the American retaliation.

About fifteen minutes later, Abdullah returned and looked crestfallen. He explained to Hamid that the explosion had been caused by someone standing on a landmine. I asked what had happened to the unfortunate person and Abdullah looked at me in a puzzled way and shrugged his shoulders.

Two hours later I heard rapid machine-gun fire but realised it was all in one direction. Maybe I was near some sort of training camp.

I tried to get some rest that night and I had no more male visitors. I had also taken Abdullah's advice and locked the door from the inside. I still could not work out in what sort of place I was staying. I could tell there was some sort of hospital attached, because I had seen a few walking wounded. I was also told it was a prison. And then, of course, to add to my confusion, there was the presence of military and intelligence people.

On the Sunday morning – 30 September – at 9.30, two Afghan men were brought to my room. I was told they were two journalists from Kabul and I was very curious about them because I knew that all Western media had been kicked out. However, I welcomed them and invited them to sit down.

This was quite exciting for me, because I think most journalists have a special bond wherever they work in the world. I had hoped these two might have agreed to sneak out some messages for me. Hamid told me to explain my story to the two men and he would translate.

About three or four minutes into my tale, I noticed that they were not taking notes or tape-recording the interview. I became instantly suspicious and could smell a rat – or even two, like the two sitting opposite me. I accused them of being impostors, or, even worse, journalists who would write only what the Taliban told them to.

I remember being very angry and I must have been gaining in confidence because I felt as though they had abused my hospitality and I ordered them out of my room. Hamid said the men were extremely important and I had to show respect, but I stood up and folded my arms and stared out of the window overlooking a beautiful garden. Just what Hamid made of me I don't know, but I think he felt uncomfortable translating for me, especially when I was in a bad mood.

After lunch that day, which had again remained uneaten, three men arrived to interrogate me. One was introduced to me as the head of intelligence. He was a very imposing-looking man with a magnificent, bushy black beard and rosy cheeks.

Most beards I saw were a bit scrawny but this one had a life all of its own. His pupils looked almost black and sharklike and I felt quite wary about this man. He looked scary, and I bet he was.

The three told Hamid they wanted to know how I had got into the country and who had helped me. They asked about the two men who were arrested at the time I was. We then went over the other questions from the previous day.

I told them that the two men had nothing to do with me and were mere fleas in the grand scheme of life. I asked why the Taliban had arrested them. They looked very irritated as though I were insulting their intelligence. The one with the bushy beard could barely conceal his irritation and I was really expecting thumbscrews or some other awful device to emerge.

Then I said that journalists were bound by a code of conduct that forbids them ever to discuss contacts or sources of information. I also reasoned that they of all people should understand because they were honour-bound to protect their guests.

The allusion to Osama bin Laden and his status as a guest of the Taliban was ignored. They couldn't even look me in the face and would stare blankly at some other spot on the ceiling. I discovered later that in Afghan culture this was a sign of respect. Hamid, on the other hand, barked several times at me, 'Look at me when I am talking to you.' He tried to get angry and aggressive but it made me laugh because I felt he was playing out of character.

Later that day a doctor arrived to give me a health check. Of course my imagination was working overtime and I thought they wanted to give me a clean bill of health before they began the torture. Anyway, this wizened little man came in and took my blood pressure. He went through the process several times and I remarked, 'Yes, yes, yes. I know. I have high blood pressure.'

Hamid gave him the gist of the conversation although I thought he understood very well in the first place. In broken English the doctor told me there was nothing wrong with my blood pressure and that it was normal. I have had high blood pressure for several years and told him so quite bluntly.

He took my blood pressure again and showed me. 'My goodness,' I declared. 'It *is* normal. You see, three days with the Taliban and I am fine. There you are, I'm very happy.' He then said something to Hamid who interrupted: 'He says you must eat or you will die.'

Abdullah came into my room with a radio and Hamid said that if I tuned in to the BBC I would hear about myself. 'You are a very high lady. You are famous. Everyone is talking about you.' The pair of them seemed to be very excited and, I as I was trying to move through the channels, I heard a soccer report that revealed that Manchester United were getting a three-nil trouncing from Tottenham.

I was so excited at hearing an English voice that I dropped the radio and I lost the station. Some more food was brought into my room but I refused to eat it and told Hamid that I would never eat again unless I spoke to my mother.

During my captivity, I managed to keep a list of dates and some brief notes, ingenuously written on the inside of a toothpaste carton. Looking back at this secret diary, which prompts me to relive the experience in my mind, I am amazed at my treatment. The entry for that particular Sunday read:

'I am given a radio to listen to the BBC World Service and am asked if there is anything else I need.'

That day's entry continues:

Hamid says everyone is very bothered that I'm not eating and asks if there's something wrong with the food, if I have a special diet or would I prefer hotel food. They constantly refer to me as their guest and say they are sad if I am sad. I can't believe it. The Taliban are trying to kill me with their kindness.

These people are in many ways like the Gurkhas. They are mild-mannered, gentle and considerate yet when it comes to fighting they are among the most fearsome warriors in the world. I wish everyone knew how I am being treated because then I could perhaps relax. I bet people think I'm being tortured, beaten and sexually abused. Instead I am being treated with kindness and respect. It is unbelievable.

Damn. I've somehow managed to break the radio so I still don't know if the world knows of my plight. I did hear a bulletin about eight Christians who have been locked up in Kabul for trying to convert Muslims to their faith.

There was to be more questioning, of course. Perhaps I should let my diary tell some of the story again . . .

Monday, October 1
The questioning goes on for hours and is very repetitive. The atmosphere is tense and I feel quite nervous. This time I am interviewed by a slim, stern scholastic-looking man and a heavy man with a red beard, and both are intimidating. Their expressions are grim as once again I try to explain why I crossed the border. Hamid is relaying my answers to them, although again I get the

impression they already understand what I am saying.

Just as I feel we are now making some progress Hamid asks again for me to explain 'exactly' why I 'sneaked' into Afghanistan.

I throw my arms into the air with exasperation and say loudly, 'Because I wanted to join the Taliban.' It was a stupid thing to say and probably the sort of comment that could get me shot and within a nanosecond of the remark spilling from my lips.

My inquisitors have, until this moment, fixed their gaze to the wall behind me. Hamid nervously begins to repeat the remark in his native Pushtu when the two men start to shake. Their shoulders begin to move and they burst out laughing to reveal a sense of humour one wouldn't normally associate with the fearsome Taliban.

It came as a happy relief to learn that my inquisitors had a sense of humour. Five minutes later, though, it was my turn to laugh when they accused me of being a secret American agent. 'If I am America's secret weapon, then God help America,' I retorted. Then I pointed out that I was sure a secret agent would have had lots of James Bond gadgets, whereas I had entered with only a Nikon camera.

They asked me what pictures I had taken and I said I had little recollection, but perhaps they should develop the film. It dawned on me that perhaps someone had opened the camera and ruined the film or, because photography is banned in Afghanistan, there would be nowhere to process it.

There were more of the same questions and my patience snapped. I told them I could not answer any more, that I had cooperated fully with them, that, once again, I was sorry for causing them hassle at a time when their minds should be fully concentrated elsewhere.

I had admitted coming into the country without a passport and visa and there was nothing more to add. I could see they were irritated but I felt the meeting ended on a fairly upbeat note and they said I should be allowed home in one or two days. 'I am happy,' I wrote in my diary, 'although I have been promised the "one or two days" release several times before.'

As I was relaxing on one of the red mattresses that I used as a bed, I heard a noise from outside. I looked out of the window and there was one of the so-called Afghan journalists with what looked like a satellite phone. He said he was staying overnight as a guest and he wanted to help me. He asked me for my mother's telephone number and said he would pass on a message to her. I refused because I said she might be more concerned if she heard a strange man on the phone saying I was fine.

I begged and pleaded to use the telephone but he refused. I then drew the curtains because Abdullah came into my room to see if I needed anything and reminded me to lock the inside of my door. He had agreed earlier not to lock my door from the outside because I had complained that maybe I needed to use the bathroom during the night. After he left I scribbled down a note to my mother saying I was fine and telling her that Nana (my late grandmother) was watching over me.

I sent my love to everyone and said to tell Dad I was being brave. I added that I hoped Daisy would remain at her boarding school, where her life would not be disrupted. The note was harmless but it contained things that I knew would ease her pain. I went back to the window and pushed the note through a hole in the outside mosquito net. The man with the satellite phone happily took it and I indicated that, if the note got through, then I would give him a real story to tell.

I hope he is genuine [I wrote] but you never know. I just wish I could speak to my mother and find out how Daisy is. It is her birthday on Wednesday and she will be expecting a card and a present. I wish I knew what was happening in the outside world and if the bombing has started yet. I feel so isolated and I wonder if anyone out there, other than my family, really cares about my situation.

I wish the mosquitoes would leave me alone. My ankles, face and wrists are covered in bites. I am so itchy I could peel my skin. I've hunted high and low and just can't find the damned things. Got really bored today and now know that the room is about seven yards long by five yards, and the fan given to me yesterday turns seven times in a minute, 420 times and hour and . . .

Yvonne, get a life. I wonder if I'm cracking up. I feel sort of normal but this is not a normal situation. I wonder what is happening at work, if I still have a job. They must know by know my little venture failed miserably. I just wish they knew how close I came to getting out.

I am spending hours staring out of the window, into the beautiful gardens surrounding this place. I don't believe it's a police station but it's not a military place, either. There's a beautiful little stream which winds round the garden and glistens in the sunlight. I wish the SAS would rescue me because I reckon they must be somewhere in the country. I wonder if they've been told of my situation and are practising getting me out.

I wonder if I could escape. They've let me keep the burka. Maybe I could sneak out in the middle of the night. Too risky, but if it becomes dangerous for me here I might have no option. God what a mess.

What a mess indeed!

8

PRAYERS, POMEGRANATES AND PRISON

The following day the mood of the questioning took a different swing and for some reason the Talibs became more interested in the male members of my family. They asked me for my grandfather's name on my father's side and I couldn't remember. They were astounded and obviously thought it most disrespectful. 'But he died long before I was born,' I protested.

The direction of the questioning had also changed and they seemed to be looking at some sort of file and checking for references. I was completely perplexed and quite scared because I couldn't fathom what information the Taliban could have on me. I had never been to this country in my life until the previous week.

They asked me if I had ever visited Iran and I shook my head. What a bizarre question, I thought. I had wanted to visit Iran, and I had wanted to go last year with Daisy, but I was told the regime would not tolerate single mothers and it would be too dangerous because I could end up being stoned by Islamic fundamentalists.

It was the Tuesday, 2 October, and there were three or four questioning me this time. It was quite disorientating. After they left Hamid returned and I began to wonder if he wasn't an intelligence officer as well. He didn't have the turban and his beard was a bit sparse but sometimes he really scared me.

'You are in serious trouble,' he told me. 'You have not told us the truth about your life. You did not tell us about your daughter. Her name is Daisy. There are lots of things you have not told the Taliban and this is very bad news for you.

'I want to help you but if you do not tell me the truth then I cannot help you. You refuse to talk about the two men who were arrested with you. Well, they are being beaten and tortured.'

I felt sick. I couldn't trust Hamid and I certainly was not going to take him into my confidence. However, I remember saying, 'You never asked me if I had a daughter. I said I was single and you moved straight down the form. I no longer live with Daisy's father. Don't you understand the concept of separation in this country?'

I explained further. 'Her father is Palestinian. He is a Sunni Muslim and his name is Abu Hakim or Daoud Zaaroura. Have a look in your history books and you will find what a great warrior he was.'

I was unashamedly using his name to get me out of this hole. I felt sure that would secure my release, but he didn't even look surprised when I mentioned David's name. Something was going on and I didn't know what. He asked me again about the two men and repeated that they were being beaten and tortured.

'Do what you want with them,' I said. 'They're nothing to me. If you get excitement from torturing innocent people, so be it. I shall have a good story to write when I get out. Tell *that* one to your Taliban friends.'

He looked shocked and disappeared. I was left alone for the rest of the day, and that was even worse, in some ways, than being interrogated. Maybe I had gone too far and now I was going to be hurt. It was like playing a game of snakes and ladders and, just as I felt I'd won one point, I went crashing down on another.

In the entry for 2 October, my diary begins to reveal the depth of my despair:

It is now 7 p.m. and I have been virtually ignored all day. There's growing tension in the air and I think I must be doomed. No one can look me in the face when they come to bring and take back the food. I am confused, and very, very scared.

Something is in the air. It's becoming quite obvious to me now that I am not going home. I wonder if they are going to kill me. I have to do something because I am now becoming very paranoid. There's an old, rusty razor blade in the bathroom. Maybe I should take it and hide it in my soap. If I am going to die I want to decide on the method myself. But how can they be so nice to me if they are going to kill me? Where are Abdullah and Hamid?

I've just slipped out of my room and knocked on the director's door opposite. I've woken up a grumpy man who dismissed me with a look of contempt and a wave of the hand. I've never seen him before but he gives me the creeps. I've told him I need to speak with the director.

What a night it has been. After I went to the director's room Abdullah and Hamid came rushing in to see me saying they'd heard I was requesting a doctor. Their faces were full of concern and I said I was OK but I needed to talk to the director, not the doctor. I told Hamid that it had become obvious to me that I was not going to leave Afghanistan and that I needed a lawyer to sort out my final will and testament.

He looked at me strangely and then left the room. Half an hour later the director came in to see me with Hamid and asked me what I wanted.

I told him about the lawyer request and said it

was a basic human right and he could not refuse me.

I choke every time I reach that passage. It's because of the razor blade. I saw it on the side of the bath every day, but this day I took it. It was a Pakistani-made blade with the trademark name of Vejay. I felt I had to take it because it would give me an extra bit of control and it would give me the decision over if and when to take my life.

I am not a suicidal person but I think I would rather bleed to death than be stoned to death or tortured beyond pain. This probably sounds ridiculous now, in the cold light of day, now that I am home and safe. But look back a moment to 11 September. It is probably an unfair comparison to make, but some office workers at the World Trade Center preferred to leap to their deaths rather than be burned in that hell that had visited them so suddenly out of the blue sky. I also needed a choice, and so slipped the Vejay blade into the tablet of Turkish soap they had provided on my first day.

The next day was another roller-coaster day. It had started very well, when I was given new clothes. I had worn the orange dress and trousers day and night for nearly seven days, so you can imagine how sweaty and smelly I was. Forgetting cultural and religious differences, I gave Abdullah a big hug when he handed over the clothes, and he smiled, but looked a bit surprised at such an immodest gesture. One of the outfits was a brown and cream cotton dress with brown trousers, but the other seemed extremely elaborate for normal prison wear. I suspected it was a wedding dress – and my suspicions were to be confirmed later.

That day was also sad for me because it was Daisy's ninth birthday. I sang to her, closed my eyes, wrapped my arms around myself and concentrated hard, trying to give her a hug. I could see her very well in my mind but I began to wonder whether I would ever touch her again. I also wondered how much she would remember of me, and whether she would ever recall our last conversation.

I had told her that whenever she needed me she just had to shut her eyes and I would be there for her mentally. The memory made me feel weepy and very sad, because nothing was really in my control – only negative and potentially damaging things such as the razor blade and the hunger strike. Something happened then that was best described in my diary entry for 3 October:

Absent-mindedly, I start fidgeting with a string of beads on my new cream and brown outfit bought for me by my captors. Suddenly I have a piece of string and three little baubles in my hand. I look down and I am reminded of the Holy Trinity – God the Father, God the Son and God the Holy Ghost. I'm not sure what prompts me but I say the Lord's Prayer and ask for help.

Suddenly I feel all the fear slowly drain from my body and I feel incredibly strong. It is a deeply spiritual moment, although those who don't know me will probably roll their eyes heavenwards.

From that moment on I decide I am going to be the prisoner from hell and withdraw all co-operation and refuse to answer any more questions. At 7 p.m. I am told I am going home tomorrow and I will be flying out with a group of Christians who have previously been charged with trying to convert Muslims.

My spirits lift and I thank God for answering my prayer.

The following day I was up at 5.30 a.m. I know because Hamid had lent me his watch. I was really excited and I couldn't believe God had answered my prayers so swiftly. I had felt a little guilty because I'd messed up the ending of the Lord's Prayer and couldn't remember the 'deliver us from evil' bit, which should have had a special significance bearing in mind my dire circumstances.

Hamid and Abdullah came in and gleefully showed me a Pashtun newspaper, which I referred to as the *Taliban Bugle*. There, on the front page, were two pictures of me. One was the head shot that the *Sunday Express* had sent to the world's media, and another one was of me standing in front of that NO FOREIGNERS BEYOND THIS POINT sign at the head of the Khyber Pass. Apparently, one of the Taliban's rules is that no photos of women should appear in newspapers or books. Obviously I was the exception to that rule.

'Everyone knows who you are. You are famous. Your face is everywhere in Jalalabad,' said Hamid. I asked him what the headline said and he began laughing.

'It says, "Yvonne Ridley is very happy",' he grinned. I remember having to laugh because it was so funny and obviously the doctor or someone speaking to the doctor about my blood pressure had leaked the story to the press. Perhaps the Taliban thought a story about me being 'very happy' with their hospitality would generate some positive local publicity – who knows!

Abdullah said he would drive me up to Kabul Airport and I asked Hamid if was joining us, but he said not. I agreed to eat a piece of bread, which made my two unlikely friends happy, and I bundled my possessions into a plastic bag. As I got up to go, Hamid looked down at my feet and realised I had no shoes.

'It doesn't matter. It's not problem,' I said. But he went out, and I realised that my journey to the airport was going to be delayed until they found a pair of shoes for me to wear. He came back and took an imprint of my foot and went away for about half an hour. The wait was excruciating and I began to become nervous.

The intelligence people had played quite a few mental games with me and had kept telling me I was going home and then had tricked me. They'd said I was a spy, which I knew would mean the death penalty, no questions asked. They had a file on me but they would not hand it over.

In the end I said they obviously had nothing on me and that I was a journalist. Even they had said that Express Newspapers had sent a 'high director' to negotiate my release. It all flurried around in my mind at the time but – what the hell! – I was convinced I was going home.

Hamid returned with a pair of flip-flop sandals with a logo on saying 'London'. I smiled and told him they fitted perfectly and he said, 'Congratulations!' He then told me to sit down and wait, and once again he left the room.

What happened next made my blood run cold and is best explained in my diary entry:

Hamid knocked on the door and said someone had come to see me. I think he said he was a Maulana [someone who is learned in Persian or Arabic] and I could tell by the expression on his face all was not well. A tall, slender cleric with flawless skin and narrow brown eyes entered the room and, counting his worry beads in a cal- culated fashion, he asked me what was my religion and what did I think of Islam. My mouth went dry as I told him I was a Christian but he wanted to know what sort and so I replied Protestant.

He smiled in such a sinister way I felt I was being led into a trap. I then continued that I thought Islam was a fascinating religion and admired the way its followers held such great passions and belief. I added that I would make it my business to look into the religion further on my return to London. Another smile followed and then he asked me if I wanted to convert then and there.

I panicked thinking if I said 'yes' he would think I was fickle and order that I be stoned. On the other hand I could risk execution just by saying 'no'. I thanked him for the offer but said I could not make such an important life-changing

decision while I was in such turmoil and
confusion. I thanked him again and waited for his
next question. He responded with another smile
and got up and left.

I was shaking when Hamid returned and I asked him if
everything was OK. He said to me very abruptly that I
could go, and ordered me to put on the burka before I left.
The order brought tears to my eyes as I begged him not to
make me wear it. He looked for guidance from one of the
intelligence officials, who gave a nod.

As I walked past Hamid he threw a sheet at me and
shouted, 'Put that on, then. Cover yourself.' I could not
understand why he was being so nasty towards me but I
didn't care anyway, because I was going home.

To get to the pickup truck there was a motley guard of
honour consisting of about forty Talibs. Most of them
smiled and I smiled back at all of them as I walked by. I
then noticed the two men who had been arrested with me
and studiously ignored them. I felt bad. They were
clamped in irons and the little girl was sitting in the back,
too.

I stepped up and into the front seat of the pickup truck
with two armed Taliban guards and the scholastic-looking
intelligence officer. It was a deeply emotional moment but
I managed to hold back my tears. Abdullah even spoke his
first English when he shouted, 'Goodbye!' I wondered if he
knew English all along. I looked back at the 'house of
tricks', as I called it, and as we pulled away the tears freely
flowed down my cheeks.

'Mam,' I said to myself, 'I'm coming home.'

The journey to Kabul was hellish and took more than six
hours. I saw beautiful green planes, rivers and reser-
voirs, dramatic landscapes, magnificent mountains and
literally hundreds of foxholes and caves. I believed that
President Bush's threat to 'smoke them out' was highly
unrealistic.

The landscape changed to barren wastelands of rubble and scorched earth. In parts it looked like that last place on God's earth. We stopped several times so the men could pray and carry out their toilet needs. No one bothered to ask if I needed a break, and once again I realised that women in Afghanistan are not even considered. 'I obviously don't need to pee because it's not yet dusk,' I said to myself.

I was allowed to smoke and, although the Afghan cigarettes they had bought me were really strong, I was grateful. As with most nicotine addicts, it was a case of 'any port in a storm' and they did the job. During the journey the driver stopped and bought a bundle of sugar cane and some pomegranates.

The sugar cane was refreshing but was soon gone. Then one of the Talibs peeled the fruit and emptied the juicy bits into a large paper bag. I remembered how, when I was a child, Mum used to give us a pin and half a pomegranate and it would keep us occupied for hours, picking out and eating the little juice-filled gems. But this was a far more satisfactory way of eating the fruit. When I told them the name 'pomegranate' they burst out laughing. I didn't think it that funny and wondered where the name originated. The driver offered me some chewing gum, which I gladly accepted.

So there I was smoking my fags and chewing gum – my mum would have been horrified. Halfway through the journey the driver stuck his gum on the dash and left it there in the baking heat while he crammed his mouth full of the pomegranate fruit. About half an hour later he popped the gum back in his mouth but it had become so sticky that part of it wrapped around the steering wheel before it reached his lips and the trail stuck to his beard. Within two minutes I was roaring with laughter at this spectacle because he had the stuff all over the place – on his hands, hair, beard, everywhere.

He stopped the vehicle, cursing deeply, and everyone else laughed. I gave him the sheet that Hamid had thrown at me and let him use it. After all, I had no more use for it because I was going home – or so I thought.

We continued our journey on the road to Kabul after the chewing-gum incident, but each metre brought pain and discomfort because we were driving through rubble, with deep, spine-jarring potholes caused by past bombings and sheer neglect. Children sat by the dusty roadside and tried to fill in the potholes with their bare hands and trowels in the hope of earning a few Afghani notes. Where the kids came from or where they lived was not clear.

We passed several villages of single-storey, mud-lined bricks. The scenes reminded me of one of those illustrated in the children's bible that was given to me when I was ten. Other villages were completely empty and looked half bombed and deserted from previous ages. I felt as though I were travelling back in time and I remembered a companion once telling me that the Taliban's aim was to create a country reminiscent of when Allah walked the earth.

Their brutal and ruthless drive to create the 'perfect Muslim state' seemed like madness to someone like me, who was brought up with television, telephones, running hot and cold water, music, dancing and singing.

About an hour into our journey the vehicle stopped and one of the soldiers got out and unclamped Jan, who then sat in the back next to the scholastic-looking intelligence officer. He tapped me on the shoulder and said, 'Don't worry. You will get a fair trial.'

I turned around and spat, 'I don't know who you are and I wish you would leave me alone.' Minutes later, from the corner of my eye I saw the officer nudge Jan and he tapped me on the shoulder again: 'How is your daughter? Do you have a picture you keep of her?'

I had shown Jan a picture of Daisy but that was left with all my valuables with Pasha. Sensing a trick I replied, 'I don't know what you're talking about. Now please leave me alone.'

We continued the journey in silence and then Jan was nudged again after some furtive whispering. 'You must not be afraid. We are all your friends.'

That was it. I threw my hands up and said, 'Stop this bloody truck. I'll bloody well walk to Kabul on my own if I have to.'

After half an hour they stopped the truck and Jan was returned to the back and clamped in irons again. I felt bad but we had a story to stick to and the only way I could move on was by maintaining that story. For all I knew they might have confessed to everything, but at the same time I could not be sure.

Afghanistan is like its people, I reflected, as we passed more dramatic landscapes. It is a country of contrasts and its people too swing from being generous and kind one minute to being hard and brutal the next.

By the time we reached Kabul it was evening and I could hardly distinguish anything. It certainly was not like a capital city. I was looking hard for the airport and we swung into a grand-looking building, which turned out to be some sort of government structure. The intelligence officer went inside. He returned after about ten minutes and said something to the driver.

We travelled about another five minutes and then entered a fortress-type building, which turned out to be the terrorist wing of Kabul Prison. There were many low points during my time with the Taliban and this was one of the most grim, but the gallows humour was, as ever, present.

I was taken through this rickety gate and into a courtyard. It was dark and I was led down a grimy corridor leading into a large – but just as bleak – corridor. In front of me was a metal door about a metre and a half (or roughly 5 foot 4 inches) high and this man wearing a black turban, who turned out to be the prison governor, pushed it open.

I peered inside out of curiosity and there were two Afghan women sitting down cross-legged on the floor with a screaming, undernourished-looking child. I looked back at the governor and the intelligence officer, and they motioned me to go in. I looked aghast and unfurled the most abusive tongue-lashing I'd dished out so far.

'You must be joking,' I said. 'I am *not* going in there. I am going home on a Red Crescent plane. I am not going into that cell. I don't do squalor: I am a British journalist and you cannot treat me like this. When I get home I will write about you – and you.' And I jabbed my finger at each one of them.

Warming to the theme, I continued: 'I demand to be put in a hotel. My newspaper will pay for it. Do you think I'm crazy? You are a set of lying bastards. You told me I was going home.'

For two men who said they didn't speak English they understood my tirade very well. The intelligence officer, who looked delighted to see me starting to crack after all his nasty mind games, said, 'This is Afghanistan. You have broken our laws. You have entered our country illegally. You will stay here.'

I was very frightened and very angry, which is so dangerous a combination for anyone to cope with that I continued screaming at the top of my head: 'I am not staying here. Don't you understand? I am civilised, I am British, you cannot do this to me.'

Just then another cell door opened and six women in Afghan dress peered outside to see what all the fuss was about. One woman, who had dark hair and glasses, asked, 'Are you from the Red Cross?'

I looked around and, still angry, snapped back, 'Of course I'm not, but I *am* bloody cross and, and— You speak English.' I stopped in mid-flow and was surprised.

The woman replied, 'Yes, I'm Australian, these two are American and the other three are German.' Happily for the Talibs, and probably for me, I had been distracted and suddenly the recognition flashed across my face as I said, 'Oh, my God! You're the Christians. But I was told you were all living in hotel rooms and had television, videos and computers.'

My remark brought laughter and giggles and they said they were humanitarian aid workers for the German-based Shelter Now International charity and that they and their two male colleagues were facing trial, charged with converting Muslims to Christianity. I asked them if they spoke Pushtu and they all did, which I thought was really impressive. I begged them to tell the two Talibs that I was not going to stay here and that they had better book me into a hotel or suffer the consequences.

Kathe, one of the German women, looked at me as though I were mad, and probably repeated my sentences, but very much toned down. The two men had a conversation with the girls and the Australian, Diana (which in her case was pronounced 'Deanna', I was to be told), said, 'You're better off staying with us tonight and we'll sort something out for you in the morning. Don't worry.'

I barked some insults at the two men before I went inside the cell, which was about 7 metres by 5 metres – or 23 feet by 16. I sat down and cried and then asked if anyone minded if I smoked. They all did! Huh, so much for Christian understanding. I said I would have a ciggy later and we sat and talked.

I realised that I had not been in the company of women for about seven days, or in that of anyone who spoke English fluently. It was actually a great comfort and a joy to find these women. I told them I was so angry that I had finally cracked up in front of those bastards and I told them my tale.

They were appalled that I had been held in the company of men only for nearly a week and said it flew in the face of the Taliban edicts. I told them I had been on hunger strike for the best part of a week and Diana said that some of them had fasted for twenty days.

Her use of the words 'fast' and 'twenty days' made me feel unworthy, so I declared that I would have a dirty protest and not wash until I was released.

'No, you will not,' Diana laughed. '*She's* doing that already, and having one stinky person in a confined place is enough!' she remonstrated, indicating Heather, one of the Americans. She made her point firmly but in a pleasant enough way, and I realised she was seen as the leader of the little group.

They were about to start one of their evening meetings, so I decided to nip out into the courtyard for a smoke. As I looked towards the heavens I watched the stars and tried to see if I could spot the satellite again, but I couldn't. I had three cigarettes, one after another, and cursed the men from Jalalabad. They had all waved me off saying I was like a sister and yet they must have known that I was going to end up here.

They had lied and lied and lied and when I was becoming resilient to their promises of freedom the bastards had caught me out again. Just then a melodic sound wafted from the prison cell and it was the girls, singing really beautiful songs. How weird is this! I thought as I stood in the courtyard of Kabul Prison. It's surreal.

I returned to my cell and we talked a while longer. I told the women that my game plan was to be the prisoner from hell and as abusive as I possibly could be. As much as I loved their company I would also insist on having my own cell because I didn't want any of my bad behaviour impacting on them.

They told me the anger would subside and I just said I could not afford to let it because I could not conform. 'If I conform then it means I am accepting my surroundings, and I don't want to become institutionalised,' I reasoned, probably sounding completely insane.

Diana looked at me and nodded, but I think she'd either experienced it or heard it all before. She asked me where I was from originally and I said near Newcastle. She said she had a friend called Doreen who was a midwife in County Durham.

'Don't worry, when I get out of here I will track her down and get her to send you a letter,' I said. I half caught myself and then added, 'That's assuming I *am* going to get out of this place.' I then remembered I needed the toilet and I was shown to a squatty potty.

'Try not to put loo roll down it because it blocks the drains,' Diana warned me. 'We use a plastic bag to deposit the paper – unless it's too bad.' That was it. I had no flush toilet and, although this one was clean, I felt I just couldn't sink any lower.

When I returned to my cell I lay down in my clothes and pulled a quilt over me. There's no such thing as night-clothes over there. You sleep in what you wear during the day. I never saw any towels, either. In Jalalabad I'd had to dry myself with a plain sheet after showering.

Abdullah would guard the door to the bathroom and the men would have to wait patiently while I showered and used the toilet. Both were in a disgusting state, and I never saw any bleach or cleaning fluids. I didn't want to clear up after that lot, either. I thought: They don't want women working? Well I'm damned if I'm going to get on my hands and knees and scrub this place out for them.

I silently cried myself to sleep that night, still feeling angry and betrayed by those men in Jalalabad. They had lied to me and must have laughed behind my back as I walked out of the intelligence headquarters. I resolved to become more awkward than ever and be the Queen Bitch from Hell. The Talibs had gone too far.

I remember thinking that it could be – and probably *would* be – a risky game plan, but if I accepted my situation I could end up in that squalid hell hole for many years to come.

9

BOMBS OVER KABUL

My first full day in Kabul Prison started off very badly. I opened my eyes and in the dim light I saw a wooden ceiling with beams and thought for a moment that I was in a ski lodge or log cabin. I was quite disorientated and thought I must have had a bad dream and that I was actually on holiday with Daisy.

As I sat up my back creaked and I looked around and saw the three German girls lying fast asleep on their floor mattresses and behind me the other three women in their bunk beds. No, it hadn't been a dream: I was actually in a living nightmare.

And I was in Kabul Prison.

I sat up and tried to think about my surroundings. It was now Friday 5 October, exactly seven days after my ill-fated donkey ride. The first person to stir was one of the German women, Kathe (whose surname, I would later discover, was Jelinek), and she asked me if I wanted a shower. Oh, joy! I thought. She saw the look on my face and said, 'Well, er, we *call* it a shower. Follow me and I'll explain.'

I was led out to the courtyard, where she showed me how to crank out the water from what turned out to be an old zinc bucket. Naïvely, I remarked, 'And it comes out hot, does it?' She began laughing at me but not in a nasty way, and I realised the answer immediately.

So I heaved my cold bucket of water across the court-yard and she took me to some shelves just beside our cell door and pointed to a heating element that was plugged into the power supply. This whole arrangement would have been condemned as unsafe in any other country.

Half an hour later I heaved the bucket down the corridor and into the toilet area. I went back and got my soap and toothbrush, and the Chinese toothpaste I'd also been given at my other place. I stripped to my flip-flops and began to wash myself, and I just stopped in time to remember the razor blade I had slipped into the soap. What a bloody stupid place to hide it, I thought.

I shuddered as I thought about the damage I could have done to myself with that thing! As I dug it back out, I reflected that I was probably more of a danger to myself than the Talibs were. I dried myself with a small blue hand towel the girls had given me.

The rest of the women, two Americans Heather Mercer and Dayna Curry, the feisty Australian Diana, whose surname is Thomas, and the two remaining Germans, Silke Durrkopf and Margrit Stebner, were beginning to stir. I pulled out my belongings and one of them exclaimed, 'Why on earth did they buy you a wedding dress?' I looked at the white chiffon and gold dress and laughed. I told them the story about the cleric asking me if I wanted to convert to Islam and I joked that maybe they had a husband lined up for me. If that was the case, I added, then some poor man in this damned country has had a very lucky escape.

They were shocked and amused when I told them I'd been there and done that *three* times – and God help Husband Number Four! There was a sort of gallows humour here similar to what I had encountered in Jalalabad and it was useful therapy for all of us.

I told them about my game plan to become the world's most difficult prisoner and they urged caution – but my mind was set.

Diana is a qualified nurse and I showed her some nasty rashes I had acquired since my captivity. She thought I had scabies, bed bugs, fleas or a heat rash. Poor Kathe had had lice from the previous prison they had been kept in, which sounded horrendous. They had had to deal with all those itchy things as well as mice, rats and bloody scorpions. The last of that lot would have freaked me out.

To my consternation they told me that the women there were regularly flogged with electric flex for no apparent reason, but that they had not personally been abused. They also said the prison staff at this particular establishment were relatively nice and harmless.

Thankfully, on closer inspection, Diana said she thought I'd suffered a heat rash from my bra. I then said I had not been to the toilet properly since I had arrived in Afghanistan and asked her if she had anything for constipation among the medical supplies they seemed to have stored in one cupboard.

'Well if you've been on hunger strike all this time you've probably got nothing inside your system,' she said.

However, I pointed out that, before I had set off on my project, I had stuffed myself like a pig at the hotel's buffet. I then recalled what I had said to the restaurant manager: that I didn't know where my next meal was coming from. I had only been joking but it took on a different resonance now.

Diana offered the choice between some fizzy laxative drink given to them by American Embassy officials and suppositories. Hmm, the decisions you have to make when you're in prison! In the end I decided to go for the suppository because I could control that, whereas laxatives – well, you just never know. And, if I was hauled off for another long interrogation, my system might decide to go into overdrive at the most inconvenient time.

Margrit said I couldn't possibly wander round dressed like a bride, so she gave me a pair of navy-blue trousers and matching top, which fitted quite well. I went and changed and got out the zinc bucket and began to wash my knickers, bra and brown and cream outfit using a pumice stone. It was a bit of a novelty at first, but I knew that I would soon tire of doing this day in and day out if it were part of everyday life.

I hung up my clothes on the washing line, which stretched across the courtyard. I was told by Kathe to cover up my knickers because she said it was deemed offensive to the Taliban soldiers who kept a constant close scrutiny on the courtyard and our actions when we ventured into it. 'Stuff 'em!' I replied, and so I started as I meant to go on.

The women were expecting their lawyer that day and began to write letters for him to take to the outside world. Heartened, I wrote a note to my news editor Jim Murray hoping the Pakistani lawyer would pass it on. The last line read, 'Jim, this is a hell hole. Please help.' I hated sounding desperate and I didn't want to upset people at work more than I had to; but, hell, it was a desperate situation and *I* was desperate and it *was* a hell hole. I felt like scrawling in huge capital letters 'GET ME OUT!'

Sadly, the lawyer turned out to be a real jobsworth and refused to hand on the message. His legal sidekick said he was amazed to see me in Kabul because they were told I was in Jalalabad, and they were going to drop in and see me. 'Forget it,' I snarled. 'I want a top London lawyer and not that bloody jobsworth.'

He looked really offended and no doubt passed the message on to the lawyer, who by this time had gone into the cell for a conference with the six women and their two male colleagues. Georg Taubmann and Peter Bunch, a German and an Australian, were in another section of the prison but had been allowed round to this section for the legal conference.

I decided to spend my time walking around the courtyard making a mental note of its width and length. I then wandered around the diameter, surreptitiously kicking the wall and tapping it to find out if there were any hollows or weaknesses. Just then, Heather, who at 24 was the younger of the two Americans, came out of the cell looking visibly upset. She was in the courtyard and started to weep.

I left her alone because most times when you want to cry you want to be left alone. Just then Peter came out and gave her a stern talking to and told her to pull herself together. When will men ever learn that that is the last thing you say to a woman when she's upset?

I felt duty-bound to interject at this point and said she should be allowed to cry and get it out of her system. She was bitterly disappointed because the lawyer had said he was returning to Pakistan and she felt he should stay with them in Kabul. Heather felt he might be afraid of the bombing.

The Aussie guy said this was a load of nonsense and there would be no bombing. Once again I intervened and said, 'It is not a case of *if* but *when* the bombing starts. Of *course* there's going to be bombing and you should prepare and brace yourself for it. There are three thousand journalists sitting on the Pakistan border and their editors haven't sent them on the off chance.'

He looked at me as though I were mad, and then I pointed out that he'd been locked up for two or more months, whereas I had been in for only a week, and I had witnessed the military build-up. I am not normally a doom-monger but I am a realist, and I thought that the point of air strikes should be made very clear.

He obviously didn't agree and walked away, disgruntled. I tried to comfort Heather and told her it was perfectly natural to want to cry, and reminded her of my 'Tiny Tears' performance the night before.

The prison governor then went into the legal meeting and, I later learned, he told everyone that if they had written about me in their letters they must rewrite them and remove all such references. I found this a wee bit disconcerting. Why should I be such a secret?

I walked in and asked if everything was OK but the aid workers looked subdued. The German man, Georg

Taubmann, who was the director of the relief operation in Afghanistan, advised me to take things easy and told me I would get nowhere by being difficult and rude.

I immediately objected to this because I didn't know him from Adam and I thought he was being patronising, so I replied, 'You might be happy to accept your life in here but I am not, and I am going to buck the system. If they're going to keep me in here then I'll make every day a living hell for them. If you're not careful you'll end up institutionalised or with that Stockholm Syndrome nonsense.'

I could see that the girls were not happy with the way in which I had spoken to him. He probably is a nice enough bloke, but he rubbed me up the wrong way, just as the Aussie chap had.

Heather came out to the courtyard and handed me a Pakistani newspaper from the lawyer, which said I was a member of the Special Forces and that it had been confirmed by the Taliban's official spokesman. Serious as it was, I had to laugh. The two aid workers and the legal team left and the lawyer turned round and told me not to worry. I shouted to him, 'Just get a message through to my newspaper because I need to get a decent lawyer out here and fast.' He scowled but he had asked for it. And then I shouted, 'By the way, I am not worried. Why should I be worried? I'm getting out of here.'

Since it was a Friday I knew I wasn't going to get out of Kabul that day because, as the girls pointed out, it was the Muslims' holy day and just about everything comes to a halt.

The following day I went into the courtyard and began to practise my yoga. The rickety gate opened and in walked the scholastic-looking intelligence officer from Jalalabad, who had also accompanied me on my journey here. He told me not to worry and that I would be leaving prison soon. I just snarled at him. I couldn't trust any of them any more, not after all the mind games. He may have contributed to the tears I'd shed as I had slipped into fitful sleep on my first night at Kabul Prison, but I sure as hell was not going to let the bastard make me cry again.

The prison governor strolled over and asked me for my name to complete my registration, but I just ignored him and walked back into the cell. He followed me in and told the girls that, without my registration I would not be eligible to any food. I asked the girls to tell him in Pushtu that I was on hunger strike, and, anyway, if he didn't know my name that was his fault and would he now clear off because his questions were annoying me.

I watched his facial expressions as this was translated to him, and it went from grim to grimmer. He barked back some sort of response before walking off. Everyone looked uncomfortable and I asked Dayna what he had said. She looked very upset, and finally she whispered, 'He said you can die, then.' I laughed and told her not to be concerned – but, to tell you the truth, I felt a lump come to my throat, so I walked out and had a cigarette.

Later we talked about our situation and Heather mentioned a Canadian man who had volunteered to exchange places with her. She said she didn't know who he was but it was a nice gesture. The remark triggered off another memory from my time in Jalalabad, when I was told that the Taliban wanted to use me for a hostage exchange with someone who was being held in London.

I had brought it up during a day of interrogation the previous week. It was a strange day and so much was happening that I could not put all my thoughts down on the little piece of cardboard box that held my toothpaste tube and also doubled as my diary.

A man had interrupted the interrogation. My interrogators had all made to stand when he'd stuck his head around the door. Then he had shaken everyone's hand. It turned out that he was the military commander of the Taliban forces. Anyway, shortly after the interruption, I said I had heard they might want to swap me. They looked uncomfortable as I said, 'You know, you'll just humiliate yourself if you ask for an exchange. Ever since

Margaret Thatcher, my government has refused to enter into bargaining or negotiations to swap hostages. Don't even *think* about it.'

Then one said, 'What about your government now?'

I rolled my eyes and said, 'Do you know how happy Tony Blair is that you've locked me up? He'll just be sad that you haven't got *more* journalists inside.'

I think they were surprised by my response, or annoyed that I had dismissed the idea; or maybe they had already 'humiliated' themselves. I don't know and I suppose I never will.

My short reverie was interrupted by Heather's laughter, as she said she would love to be swapped rather than stay another day here. I had to admit that they had had a really long stint and I was full of admiration for their strength.

After the morning fiasco of having to get ready – it takes about two hours just to wash and dress without mod cons – Kathe and Silke were sitting outside in the courtyard reading and Diana was in another corner. Margrit was lying down and Dayna was reading on her bed. I think Heather was talking to the prison warden. Just then we heard anti-aircraft fire ripping through the sky and I leaped up from a rug I'd been sitting on. There were all sorts of heavy-artillery noises and Heather just lost it and started running around, screaming in Pushtu for the prison governor and the two male aid workers.

I hadn't a clue what the hell was going on but I knew that she was panicking and such actions could affect us all. Frightened that we would be locked in a cell I grabbed hold of her and said, 'Shut up and listen to me, Heather. This could be help on the way, and the last thing we need is for you to be running around like a blue-arsed fly. You have to get a grip and I will help you.' But she just pushed me away and continued running around.

I went over to Diana and begged her to do something because we all had to stick together. This could the start of a Special Forces operation and, if they were going to get us out, we would have no more than twenty seconds. She said Heather was fragile and she could not control her when she panicked.

The prison governor arrived and then he called for the two men. The Aussie bloke, Peter, was telling Heather to calm down but she said she wanted us all to go in a bunker, and that was the last place I wanted to be. He tried to calm her and said it was just an air-raid practice. Now, while I'm all for trying to keep the peace, I don't believe in blatant lies. 'I'm sorry, mate, you don't just whack off a load of surface-to-air missiles for nothing.' Nope, we were not going to get along at all. It turned out that the Americans had sent up two of their drones, or unmanned spy planes, over Kabul.

Thankfully, it all calmed down and the two men went back to their cells. Later I told Heather she must not panic again because none of us wanted to be put in a bunker. The others agreed and I think she was hacked off, but her behaviour had concerned me.

I was convinced the SAS would come and get us out and I told her this, but she was horrified at the idea. I told her that, if she insisted on hiding in a bunker when the bombing started for real, she might find herself on her own, and I could see that that disturbed her. After all, she was just 24 years old and it was a great load for her to deal with. However, I am not that brave a person and I didn't relish having my life jeopardised by someone having a panic attack.

Thankfully, there was some cheer just around the corner when post arrived for Heather and Dayna. Heather said triumphantly that her father had written to her and told her not to worry, and that America would hold off its military campaign until she was safe and sound. This exasperated me and I told her so. She became very defensive and said her father, who was staying in the American Embassy, would not lie to her. I replied, 'I'm sure he wouldn't, and nor would you want him to. However, I cannot think that Colin Powell will take your father into his confidence and tell him when the bombing's going to start, especially when he knows that he's writing to you in a Taliban prison.'

I was sorry to be the bearer of bad news but, as I say, I was being realistic, and prison is not a place for pipe dreams. Anyway the mail did cheer up her and Dayna, and I think Kathe got a letter that had her very excited, because the German girls got hardly any mail. It all had to be translated into English and I guess that was too much for the Taliban to deal with.

Silke didn't receive any post and it had a very bad effect on her because she was already feeling down. She went out of her cell and shed a few tears. This unnerved me because Silke was very strong and normally in control. She got it out of her system and remained in the courtyard for a while. I think her tears had affected the prison governor, who had delivered the letters, because it was totally out of character for her. I suppose he was an old softy, really, but I wasn't going to cut him any slack.

Later in the day two men from the Foreign Ministry arrived with the grim-looking prison governor and announced that I was now the guest of the Foreign Ministry, and that I no longer had anything to do with the intelligence department. I was relieved because it meant all this dangerous talk of spying and special forces might be over.

I had just finished my second session of yoga for the day, which I had taken to doing during the midday sun and around 4 p.m. because I wanted the Taliban to think that I was either an amazingly strong woman or barking mad. Either way, I think they found the whole display disturbing, and had been huddled in the corner until I opened my eyes.

After breaking the good news to me, they then said they needed to ask me a few questions and it would probably take no more than a couple of hours. I went ballistic, refused to cooperate and told them they could all go to hell. As I launched into my second offensive I had my hands on my hips and I was tapping my foot. One of the men, called Mr Afghani, whom I always referred to as the Smiling Assassin, said those fateful words that I had heard so many times in Jalalabad: 'But you are our guest and we want you to be happy.'

I screamed at him, 'I am not your bloody guest: I am a prisoner. I cannot walk out of this place. Countries are often judged on the quality of their prisons and this place is a squalid hell hole, which makes you primitive, cruel people. You disgust me.'

His associate said defensively, 'But what do you expect? This is Afghanistan. We have been at war for twenty-two years and our prisons are not a great priority. You have been bad and came into our country uninvited.'

I waved him down dismissively and told them again to go to hell and get out of my sight. With that I walked up to them, spat at their feet and returned to the cell. The girls were gobsmacked by what they saw and heard and urged caution. I have to admit that this time I felt I had gone too far and I became deeply afraid. As I stood there I could feel myself quaking and I wanted to be sick. My stomach felt as though it contained a thousand butterflies.

Heather, who was quite friendly with the prison staff, walked over and one of the women warders stood in the doorway glaring at me. 'They say you might get beaten or flogged if you speak to important people like that. I just thought I ought to warn you.' Of course at this point most sane people would have just shut up but I must have been insane because I replied, 'If I am beaten and I feel pain then I will be happy because I will know I am still alive.'

Such strong, brave words. Which B movie did *they* come from? I wondered. The reality was quite different. I was even more afraid and still shaking inside as I waited to be hauled off and beaten with a hose – a common occurrence for the local prison population.

About twenty minutes later, the rickety gate went and I heard male voices. Heather dashed back into the cell in a panic and said that the Smiling Assassin had returned with the other man. I felt my legs wobble and I tried to brace myself as I heard their voices approach the cell door.

Three of the girls threw themselves to the floor and grabbed hold of me desperately praying for God to give me strength, and begged him to help me so I wouldn't feel any pain from torture. I know they meant well but I felt as though I were trapped in a scene from Monty Python's *The Life of Brian*. The power of prayer had helped me in Jalalabad, and I'm not sure whether God was there for me again, but, to everyone's amazement, Mr Afghani had a satellite phone in his hands and not a piece of electric flex. He told everyone that they could telephone their relatives. They were so excited and, one after another, chatted away. It was especially emotional for the German girls and Diana, because they had not spoken to anyone since they were arrested. It was just the sort of fillip Silke needed as well.

I, of course, was excluded and Kathe, bless her, asked Mr Afghani if I could also speak to my parents. 'She cannot call anyone. She is uncooperative and bad. Did you know she spat at us?' Although I was sad not to speak to my family I was still very happy for the women. They deserved a break.

Bad news or news of bad tempers travels fast in Afghanistan, and the next day the deputy foreign minister, a small, round, jolly-looking man, came to see me to tell me that I would be out soon. I was quite dismissive but he told me not worry. 'I'm not worried: I'm just bloody angry,' I told him. 'Your words are dust and I can trust no one after being so badly betrayed about my journey to Kabul. The intelligence people lied and lied, and now I'm here. This is a hell hole.' I was shouting by now. 'What sort of people *are* you?'

We were in the courtyard and the prison governor looked over in disgust. I returned to my blanket and continued my yoga. The sun was overhead and the heat was blistering. As I sat down I waved at him and said, 'You can go now.'

I was very puzzled and mentally exhausted. It seemed as though I could be as rude and abusive as I wanted but I couldn't get a reaction from them other than a smile and the usual bollocks about being their guest. It was really tiring being Mrs Angry all the time and I didn't know how much longer I could keep up this act. I am not an aggressive, rude person by nature, either, so it was also difficult to play out of character all the time.

Heather offered me the Ken Follett novel, *Code to Zero*, to read. 'We've all read it and it's fantastic,' she enthused. 'I promise you won't be able to put it down.' I declined because I felt that, if I was going to read a lengthy book, it would mean that I had accepted that I was going to be here for a long while.

Margrit said I could read *her* book when she wasn't using it. It was a series of short stories, so I could dip in and out as the mood took me. I looked at it and started laughing at the irony of it all. The book was a compilation by that disgraced political rogue Jeffrey Archer. I told the girls he was in prison but I bet *he* didn't have to hand-crank his water every morning.

I wondered if he would get out before I did. Then we started talking about the Western hostages who had been held in Beirut – including Terry Waite, Terry Anderson and John McCarthy – and I thoroughly depressed myself when I remembered how long they were held in captivity. I told Heather that, by comparison, we were well off in Kabul Prison – and at least we could wander around.

However, prison life is still mundane and routine. It's even more boring when you're not eating. The women supplemented their basic prison diet of bread and rice by making a daily shopping list for fresh food and provisions, which they handed to a female prison warder. Like most foreign prisons, if you have the requisite money, arrangements can be made to buy in food from outside. Dayna had the cash and all the women took turns to cook. Although I was no longer having hunger pangs, and had stopped salivating at the thought of eating, I remember

Silke cooking a meal one day and the aroma was beautiful. She also cut up fresh coriander leaves and the smell seemed to fill the air. If I close my eyes and concentrate I can still smell it.

That night I found it difficult to get to sleep because the baby in the end cell was forever screaming. I was told the two Afghan women with it were locked up because they had invited strange men into their home who wanted to buy an Afghan carpet from them.

Women in Afghanistan had no life under the Taliban regime. Mind you, their lives had not been that much better under the previous lot. It is so sad that women are totally overlooked in this country and have no other role in life than to have babies. Of course, we saw women defiantly showing their faces in public as the Taliban began to be routed during mid-November, but how the quality of their lives will shake down in the long term remains to be seen.

The man from the Foreign Ministry returned later in the day and told me that soon I would have my own cell. 'We just want you to be happy, you are our guest,' he said. I was about to protest again but he then hastily added, 'We know you have experienced similar conditions in Iran, so we don't know why you call us primitive.' He had the sort of look on his face that said he'd just revealed or hinted at some great secret. Lord knows what he was talking about because I have never been to Iran in my life.

I had very little knowledge about what was happening outside Kabul Prison, other than that my newspaper was continuing to have a series of meetings with the Taliban ambassador in Islamabad. I wondered whether the *Express* chairman Richard Desmond was trying to organise an 'at-home-with-bin-Laden' exclusive called 'My Cave' for *OK!* magazine, which he also publishes.

The prison governor was talking to one of the girls and apparently he said, 'I've got George Bush on my back over you girls and now Tony Blair is asking about that awful Englishwoman.'

I was overwhelmed because I really didn't think that I was that important and hoped that there wasn't too much of a fuss being made back home. Then I was shown a Pakistani newspaper that said I was a member of the Special Forces. I shouted to the women, 'Oh, we're OK, girls. I'm in the SAS and I'll get you out tonight by the inflatable helicopter I've buried in the courtyard.'

It was just another example of the black humour that seemed to give me strength, but I was deeply concerned at the content of the article and wanted to wring the bloody journalist's neck. I felt he had signed my death warrant. Somehow I just had to bury these rumours.

I had two secrets that could cost me my life. The Taliban would never understand why I had married an Israeli (Husband Number Three) – and to tell you the truth I couldn't understand why I married him either. For that I should be flogged. The other was the fact that I had been in the Territorial Army.

We were told to stay in our cells because some men were coming round to clear out a cell for me and we must hide from them. This was all very tiring and I'd been here only a few days, but already I was beginning to feel like a third-class citizen because I was a woman.

I went to inspect the cell later and it looked disgusting. The concrete floor had a huge hole in the corner and I saw a rodent of some sort dive down it as I wandered in. There was a big religious mural on the wall with lots of Arabic writing and windows overlooking the men's prison.

I looked at the door. It was of solid metal with a lock and I had this sudden fear that I would be locked inside every time I was abusive, which could be 24 hours a day. I asked the girls if they had any superglue so I could damage the lock. In the end I managed to break it using a piece of stone and some dirt.

The jolly man from the Foreign Ministry arrived with the prison governor and he asked me what I thought of the cell. It told him it was inadequate and I wouldn't put an animal in it, not even in Afghanistan. To my surprise he agreed and apologised for the 'squalid' and cramped conditions I had been forced to live in.

He told me to collect my belongings because he wanted me to move into a more comfortable room in the Taliban sleeping quarters. I was quite suspicious of this softening of attitude and wondered whether I was going somewhere awful to be tortured. He kept saying I would be released in the morning but I just replied, 'Yes, yes. Do you know how many times I've heard that? Tomorrow, *inshallah* [if Allah wills]!'

I demanded to inspect the room first and was taken outside the courtyard and up some stairs, and was shown to a very spacious room, which looked right out to Kabul Hill. I have to say I was impressed but kept stony-faced and said it was adequate.

I went back to my old cell and said to Diana, 'There's a softening of attitude but I don't know what's going on. Maybe I *am* going home soon. Thank you for everything and God bless.' Another of the girls pushed the Follett novel into my hand and I was whisked away.

It was Sunday evening and dusk had arrived, so I switched on the light in my room. The obligatory Afghan rug was the centrepiece with cushions surrounding it and a rickety little hospital bed in one corner. For once I decided not to poke around the room because I had started reading the novel and was immediately gripped.

Suddenly, the silence was shattered by huge flashes streaming across the sky followed by tracers, anti-aircraft fire and the deafening sounds of cruise missiles hitting their targets. You can hear cruise missiles twenty miles away but these were landing within half a mile of the prison and the impact shook and rattled the windows.

I leaped off the bed and pressed my face against the windows. It was about 9 p.m. and I could see all the lights from homes on the hill: it looked so alpine and Christmassy in the dark. Without warning, we were all plunged into darkness and then eight Taliban soldiers came crashing into my room. Their actions startled me more than anything else because normally they would have knocked.

Several dived under my bed and began pulling out rocket-propelled grenades (RPGs). Christ, I thought. I've been puffing away like Fag Ash Lil less than a metre away from a bloody big stockpile of weapons. I was furious and asked them what they thought they were doing.

One who bothered to answer was laughing and pointing to the sky saying, 'Amreeka! Amreeka! Atch, atch, atch, atch, atch!' This gung-ho nonsense irritated me, so I pointed out that Kalashnikovs and RPGs were not going to knock a bloody B-52 bomber out of the sky. As they ran off with their weapons I shouted, 'You may as well use bows and arrows!'

Just then the prison governor came in and motioned me to be calm and not to worry. I wasn't worried for myself, but I *was* worried about the aid workers downstairs, in particular Heather. If she freaked out over the drone attack on the Saturday then this would really send her over the edge. I asked him to take me downstairs, but he refused.

He then left and I could have sneaked out but there was no way I was going to wander around with a bunch of wild-eyed Talibs looking for a target to fire at. You know, the fog of war and all that. So I went back to my perch and watched the bombing, which lasted about forty minutes. There were obviously two targets and I reckoned one was near the airport, where there was some sort of military training camp, and the other seemed to be a mile in the other direction.

What was totally weird was the night sky, because the only colours that were thrown up were in silver, white and shades of grey. It was all monochrome. But what was really frustrating was that the only Western journalist in Kabul to see the start of the Western bombing had no means of filing the story!

There I was with a bird's-eye view and I couldn't ring the newsdesk and tell them about the awesome sight I was witnessing. I didn't even know whether I would ever be around to describe the intermittent jets of fire going up into the air, one after the other, and other flashes coming up.

At first I felt very relieved and then I remembered the obnoxious Mr Afghani, a.k.a. the Smiling Assassin, who punched the air when he heard that the Talibs had shot down a spy plane. So in his honour I started to sing 'Rule Britannia' at the top of my voice.

I felt the adrenaline pumping through my body and I actually felt relieved that the bombing had started. It may seem very self-obsessed and self-centred, and in my defence I have to say prison does that to you, but I had had a nagging feeling that they might be holding back the bombing because of me and the aid workers.

My thoughts suddenly rushed to my family and the agony they would be going through when George Bush announced to the world that the bombing had started.

The Taliban soldiers returned and knocked on my door. As I opened it they filed in looking very subdued as they put the RPGs under my bed.

10

RETURN TO ISLAMABAD

On the morning of Monday 8 October, I was up at around 5.30 and decided to have a shower and wash my hair. I walked into the toilet and wanted to throw up – it was disgusting. It was a flush loo, but it was filthy. I made a mental note to inspect all toilets in future before agreeing to move.

I decided against the shower. I just wanted to get out as quickly as possible. I returned to my bedroom and brushed my teeth in there. I was told to be ready by 6 a.m. and there was a knock on the door. Excited, I went to answer it, but it was only someone with a piece of bread for breakfast and some green tea.

I wondered how the girls were after the bombing. I had told my fellow inmates that, while it may sound terrifying, they were quite safe, because all the targets would be terrorist targets. I remember telling Heather that the smart missiles have got such a degree of accuracy that, if they wanted to take out a tree in the next garden, they could do it without harming us.

The biggest thing we were all afraid of was the reaction of the people of Kabul to the bombing, because if they wanted revenge on America and Britain they knew which prison the Westerners were being held in. Anyway, there was nothing that night.

My mind soon returned to my own situation, and I walked on to the landing, where a few Talibs were standing talking to the prison governor. I shouted at him and threw open my arms saying, 'Well? Where's my car? Where's my driver? This is more bullshit. If you want a war, I'll give you a war. Look what's happened to Slobodan Milosovic: he's behind bars. This will happen to you and I will write about and identify every single one of you to a war-crimes tribunal.'

With that I retreated back in to my room and I slammed the door, bolting it on the inside. I was furious that once again I had been conned and once again the Talibs were playing more mind games.

Of course, looking back now, I think I must have been cracking up, because I certainly was not in a position to threaten these people with anything. I'd laughed at them the night before about using bows and arrows, but I didn't even have a pea shooter.

I remember returning to the rickety bed, looking back under it, and seeing all the RPGs. In some ways I thought this was a good sign because, if they thought I was some sort of GI Jane or Special Forces woman, they would never have left me with such weapons. Bearing in mind my gaffes with guns, could you imagine the damage I could cause with an RPG? I'd probably blow off my foot or my head.

I decided to keep myself occupied with the book given to me by the girls. They were right: I did get engrossed, but, because I had been in such a hurry to read it the previous day, when I reached the final chapter I was wondering how I was going to keep myself occupied, since it was obvious that I wasn't going anywhere.

I went for a cigarette from the box of two hundred the aid workers had bought me, which, considering they are all nonsmokers, I thought was jolly decent. To my utter dismay, I noticed I had only one match left and I obviously didn't feel like going back, cap in hand, to my captors to ask them for more.

There was only one thing for it: I lit the cigarette and chain-smoked until I felt sick. I must have smoked about seven cigarettes on the trot after I finished the book. I paced up and down the room and started singing 'Rule Britannia' again, simply because I'd remembered last year's Last Night at the Proms and I'd missed this year's event because I was over here.

Then I started belting out the National Anthem in defiant tones. I've never been able to sing and I was so upset and angry that not only was I way off tune but I was shaky. The soldiers outside probably thought: *Now* we know why singing is banned.

They no doubt thought I'd lost the plot and when I ventured near the window I looked down and caught the eyes of a smiling soldier looking up. He moved away from a dusty old car and there on the window in a handwritten scrawl through the dust were the words: 'Yu [sic] are walking from Kabul'. I smiled but I did not believe him.

I moved away again and when I returned he had written more words telling me I was going home and that he was saying goodbye and that he would miss me. I was surprised at this because I did not think we had met, but it is possible he was one of the many soldiers I entertained with my courtyard yoga and with my spectacular rows with the authorities.

I got out my pen and on a cigarette packet I wrote, 'Thank you for your kind words. I hope I am leaving and if I am then I wish you all well for the future.' I dropped the cardboard through a hole in the window and he picked it up and walked away very happy.

I wonder if Mullah Omar had a rule banning that sort of contact. Probably. He had just come out with a corker while I was inside. Women were no longer allowed to go on picnics unless a tent was erected where they could eat out of sight of men. Crazy.

By about 9.15 a.m. the jolly man from the Foreign Ministry knocked on the door and asked me to open it. I told him I didn't trust him and that he could go to hell. 'You are all liars and I'm not falling for your tricks again,' I blasted. He insisted the car had arrived and I could go, but I still didn't believe him.

In the end the knocking became more frantic and so I decided to open the door. As the bolt slipped, the blue wooden door was flung wide open and about five people barged into my room, insisted I sit down and told me that a car was waiting to take me to the border.

The prison governor handed me a beautiful, thick, black velvet dress with red and gold veil and said it was a traditional Afghan outfit. He asked me to put it on before I left. I was moved by the gift, especially because I had made this man's life a complete misery, but I said I feared I might ruin it on the six-hour journey to the border.

The jolly ministry man said, 'I was concerned for you and I came round last night to reassure you after the bombing, but when I arrived you were asleep.'

I replied, 'What bombing? Oh *that*. I thought it was a farewell fireworks party from the Taliban.' He looked at me, and then paid me a great compliment. 'Ridley, you are a man. You are a great game player. Come, now – it's time to go.'

For the first time I smiled warmly at him and apologised for my bad behaviour. I turned to the prison governor and thanked him for the dress and said that, however difficult I'd been, he must not take it personally. I insisted not all English women were as badly behaved as I was. He looked me up and down and then his stony face relaxed into a warm smile and his deep brown eyes crinkled.

With that I left, and bemused Taliban soldiers watched with interest as 'Ridley the man-woman' was led to a waiting Space Cruiser vehicle. I didn't see anyone else and we headed for the Foreign Ministry, where a diplomatic official waited to escort me to the border.

The Smiling Assassin came over to me and, while I had been kind to everyone else, I could not stand this man and maintained an expressionless face as he said, 'I hope you will not write bad things about us when you return to England. It was the intelligence people who gave you a bad time, not the Foreign Ministry.' I ignored him and for once he stopped smiling. That was quite a strong moral victory for me.

The diplomat who joined us could not speak English very well, so we were going to have a largely silent journey. We had to go to his house because he had forgotten his passport – and the irony of that one was not lost on any of us, despite our communication difficulties.

He lived in a block of flats in a nice area of town obviously used by Kabul's élite and it did not escape my notice that there were a few TV satellite aerials around this place. I was also told that the ruling class made sure their children, including daughters, received a good education in superior schools in Pakistan. Typical!

As we headed through Kabul in the daylight what I saw was a tale of two cities. One part was bombed to hell and badly scarred, and huge parts were derelict from previous wars over the years. The other revealed elegant tree-lined avenues where embassies stood empty. The Chinese flag flew high over one magnificent building.

I looked for plumes of smoke from the night before, but the whole city was just bombed out. It was so depressing. Kabul has been bombed so many times that the reaction from the locals is a bit like someone in Manchester saying, 'Oh, it's raining again.' In fact they would probably be more excited by rain. Kabul was like a ghost town – those who needed to get out had gone.

The scenery as we headed out of the city was dramatic, and driving through the Kabul Gorge was even more breathtaking for me than the Khyber Pass. I have to admit my nerve started to go on occasions as we threaded our way on minute mountain roads. Ravines and slopes were littered with vehicles that hadn't made it.

As we passed through the gorge and through huge tunnels carved into the rock I thought about the six-hour journey ahead and contemplated the rubble and debris that lay in store. At each checkpoint we passed, the diplomat waved a paper signed by Mullah Omar declaring that Yvonne Ridley was to be released on humanitarian grounds.

One group of Talibs were not happy, especially since they'd just had the hell bombed out of them the night before. They asked everyone to get out of the vehicle, but an argument ensued with the driver, who grabbed the precious piece of paper and drove off. I was frightened but relieved that he had had taken the initiative.

Halfway through our journey, we stopped at a single-storey building and, while the soldiers went in one way, I was directed in another. I thought it must be a toilet and I dashed in to find several women sitting with their children eating on an oilcloth on the floor. I asked them where the toilet was. Although they didn't seem to understand me, they pointed at a curtain. Relieved, I dashed through the curtain and came to an abrupt halt.

Two rows of about twenty men had been eating but they stopped and looked up at me. Thank God I hadn't lifted my dress up when I dashed in or I might have cleared the place, I thought to myself. I saw our party and they beckoned me over to sit with them and eat.

It was to be my first proper meal since my arrival in the country and I have to say the food tasted delicious, even though the place was swarming with flies. I later referred to it as 'the Restaurant of a Thousand Flies' when I told friends at home. It's funny how just one bluebottle can drive me to distraction as I chase it around the house, but here they were all over the place and I didn't bat an eyelid as I sat with the diplomat, the driver and two armed Taliban guards. We ate in silence and then, when we left, the men went off to pray.

I still needed to use the toilet and I remember seeing this pristine-looking shower and washroom nearby, which had been erected by the Canadian government. Why, I'm not sure, but I was jolly grateful for the hygienic facilities available. The caretaker came over to me in a very excited manner when he saw me try to get into the female section, only to find the door locked.

He had the key and was delighted to welcome me into his sparkling new toilets. I was equally delighted and dashed in. When I emerged I gave him an approving smile and he said, 'English journalist' and nodded. I'm not sure whether the guards told him or not.

Along the way, we passed caravan trains with camels and goatherds. I thought: Where are these people going to? The caravan people were absolutely beautiful and startling to look at. So diverse: very strong faces, wild manes of hair and emerald eyes, deep-hazel eyes, deep-brown eyes.

The country in parts is totally barren and bleak and it looks like the last place on God's earth. The landscape is lunar but it was just like that when I was taken to Kabul. I really couldn't see any evidence of bombing on my journey.

As we drove through Jalalabad people came up to our vehicle and shouted, 'English journalist'. It appeared that I had become a celebrity in the city where I had been paraded more than a week earlier.

The diplomat began laughing and said in faltering English, 'You are famous in these parts. Everyone knows your face.' As we headed towards Torkham we overtook a Datsun pickup truck, in which two armed men were sitting idly at the rear. They had their legs dangling lazily over the tailgate, hugging their Kalashnikovs and enjoying the last of the sunshine.

My eyes met with one of the men and I had to give a double take. This world is so small that it is frightening. There, sitting in the back was the green-eyed man who had brought my adventure to an abrupt end after the unforgettable incident with the unpredictable donkey.

He also looked at me in disbelief and the recognition was instant. The truck overtook us several times as Emerald Eyes shouted at the driver and asked where he was taking me. I momentarily feared that he was going to capture me again so I could go through the hell of it all, but he started laughing and seemed happy and content that I was going home.

They followed us for the next few miles and shouted to passers-by pointing to my vehicle. These people are amazing. No grudges, no signs of hostility, yet, only hours earlier, Britain and America had bombed the hell out of them.

As we arrived at the border dusk was approaching and we sat in front of the huge iron double gate that separated me from my freedom and the outside world. There was tension in the air and the armed guards kept people away from me.

I quietly willed the gate to open but instead I had to sit through the longest 38 minutes of my life. There had been rioting on the border some hours earlier in which three people had been killed, and there were fears that some Afghans might become hostile if they saw I was being returned less than 24 hours after the US and the Brits had blasted their country.

The Taliban soldiers were nervous, too, and eventually they got out of the vehicle and called for some reinforcements from nearby soldiers. I wondered whether this was another trick and then I was told that I couldn't be handed over because there was no one there from the British Embassy. I was devastated, and suspected it was another mind game being played on me.

The young diplomat who had returned could see the fear in my face and so, despite his orders to release me only into British hands, he took the decision to free me and for that I will be for ever in his debt. The double gate slowly opened and the car lurched forward five yards. 'You can go,' he said with a smile. I was numb.

As I stepped out I was suddenly hit by the glare of television lights shining into my face. I could not see a thing and was momentarily dazzled. A voice shouted out, 'How did the Taliban treat you?' All the memories and mind games of the last ten days flowed through my head and I replied, 'With courtesy and respect.'

I wanted to collapse and cry but I was mindful that my parents and even Daisy might be watching the television. I thought of my family and friends watching and I thought of all my mates at work watching. I just didn't want to cause anyone any more anguish and pain.

I wanted to punch the air with joy but I couldn't. Those two men and the little girl were still in Kabul along with the Christian aid workers from the German charity Shelter Now International. I wanted to say so much but I was still shattered by the delay at the gates and the news that no British representatives were here.

There was a mêlée of people and I was led gently inside to a building and up some steps into a long room, which was crowded with military brass, diplomats and journalists. I was asked what I wanted to drink and I felt like saying a large Scotch, but I remembered I had left one Muslim country for another.

The camera lights went on again and I have to say that at this point I kicked into reporter mode and realised I had a great exclusive which Express Newspapers would want.

I turned and asked the deputy chief of protocol for Peshawar if he would tell the Pakistani TV crew to stop filming because I was exhausted and did not want to talk to anyone. The crew stopped filming without any objections and I thanked them. The Pakistani reporters sitting to my right also respected my wishes and stopped firing questions at me.

Tea and biscuits. It was all very civilised, all so British – except that I was the only Brit there. The Taliban diplomat sat opposite and he smiled over at me. I think he was just relieved I hadn't badmouthed his people as I had constantly threatened to do throughout my captivity. Now he'd be able to go back to Kabul without fear of being shot or stoned.

The reality was that the Taliban had treated me with courtesy and respect, contrary to their reputation. The people with an almost relaxed capacity for barbarism had been chivalrous – which was more than I could say about the brutal and sometimes savage treatment that was soon to follow from so-called fellow journalists.

I was driven under an armed escort through the Khyber Pass and to the political agent's office. As we made the journey his deputy, Shahzada Ziauddin Ali, said, 'Don't you remember me? I gave you access to the Khyber Pass a few weeks ago. If I had known you were going to do this I would have tried to get you into Afghanistan myself. I also said no cameras were to be taken.' And at this he chuckled.

As we pulled into the office there were a few reporters and photographers standing at the entrance. They didn't give our vehicle a second glance. Once inside, I was taken to an imposing teak-panelled office where Fida Muhammad Wazir was sitting waiting for 'the troublesome Miss Ridley'. Behind him was a roll of honour listing the names of all the political agents to the Khyber Pass since the nineteenth century and there at the end was Mr Wazir's. I pointed this out and he told me that he had taken up his appointment just a few weeks before I was captured.

He leaned forward and asked, 'Who took you in and helped you around Afghanistan before you were caught?' I smiled and said that, with all due respect, if I hadn't told the Taliban for ten days then it was unlikely I would tell him. He nodded, showing neither approval nor dis-approval.

I then asked him whether any of his people had been reported missing in Afghanistan since my arrest and he shook his head. I had to do something about my two guides and the little girl but I couldn't confide in him, otherwise they would be in deeper trouble on their release.

I then added, 'Shahzada tells me I have a lot to thank President Musharraf for because I understand he helped secure my release.' He nodded and said he had put 'immense' pressure on the Taliban. I asked him to pass on my deepest and sincerest thanks.

Just then David Smith from the *Daily Express* knocked on the door and popped his head round. He looked aghast when he saw me. I suddenly felt self-conscious because I had no make-up on, my hair, still covered in a scarf, was a mess and the shalwar khameez outfit I was wearing was dusty and sweaty. Did I really look that bad?

However, the reason for David's double take was that two minutes earlier he had been told by an official from the British Embassy that growing speculation over my release was premature. ' "Don't worry, we have our people at the border and the instant she comes through you will be the first to know",' recounted David, mimicking the embassy official's voice.

He gave me a big hug and then ran out to find the agency photographers hired by the *Express* as he kicked into news-hound mode. Seconds later he was back, his mobile to his ear, while the photographer took his pictures. He then handed the phone over to me, and Chris Williams, editor of the *Daily Express*, exclaimed, 'Welcome back! When we heard, a huge cheer went around the newsroom. Everyone is *so* delighted! How are you feeling?'

I felt emotions welling inside of me and told him how great it was to speak to him – and that I was dying to have one of Lynne's Pimm's at Stammy's! I explained that I was going to give David a cracking story but also felt obliged to give a press conference to the media. I relayed my story to David and, being a reporter, I knew what bits to give him.

I sat and had another cup of tea with the political agent and he offered me some food from a very nice buffet. I enquired whether he was expecting more people and he said he was under the impression I would have been accompanied by officials from the British High Commission.

I have to say I was absolutely devastated and thought to myself: My God, something so bad has happened that they want nothing to do with me. Shahzada told me not to get upset and that he had arranged a big welcome-home party for me at his house. Later, I found out that the reason no one from the British High Commission met me at the border was because they had been expecting me much earlier and by the time I was set free it was pitch-black and impossible for the Royal Navy helicopters to fly.

I tried calling my mum but her phone was engaged. She was probably talking to Viv, because David Smith had told her I was back and would call later. Gary Trotter, a photographer with Images Sans Frontières, took loads of pictures and then David and I jumped into a waiting car. I sat in the back with another Images photographer, Aral Sedat, and we set off following Shahzada's car, but as we reached his office we were ambushed by about fifty photographers, reporters and cameramen. 'Keep your head down, and cover your face. Say nothing,' shouted David to me. I was shocked and had a sudden flashback. Very similar words and phrases had been used as I had entered the land of the Taliban.

The car rocked a couple of times and suddenly one of the hacks opened the driver's door and tried to take the keys out of the ignition to immobilise the vehicle. The driver was almost catatonic. Had he been prepared he would have driven through these callous bastards and they would have jumped out of the way, but he made the mistake of stopping.

Someone else tried to open my door and drag me out but Aral pulled me towards him and put a protective arm around me. At the second attempt to open the door David shouted, 'C'mon lads. Give her a break. She's just been in prison for ten days and we don't know how she is. She's not ready for this.'

Sympathy, that well-known word in the dictionary that comes somewhere between shit and syphilis, was not in evidence in Peshawar that night. 'Get the bitch out, she knows the game,' barked one photographer. 'She's a fucking journalist, she knows the score. Get her out now,' screeched someone else. More abuse and anger followed.

Even when I was being driven around Jalalabad, accused of being an American spy, none of the Afghans or Taliban vented this sort of fury at me. They fired their guns in the air but I thought this lot's mood was far uglier.

I really could not believe what I was hearing. Not even my Taliban tormentors had spoken to me like that. They had shown me respect, but this lot had none for me at all. It was very confusing.

Shahzada jumped out of his car and managed to beat them off in spectacular fashion. When we got into his office I was dazed and confused. David asked if I was OK and I said I was really stunned. He then tried for a third time to raise 'our man' in Islamabad. He finally got hold of Colin Mulcahy, a diplomat at the high commission, who by this time was aware that Yvonne Ridley was back in town and in the hands of Express Newspapers. He said he was on his way to take me back to British High Commission.

David then told me Paul Ashford, Editorial Director of Express Newspapers, and Salayha Hussain-Din, an Urdu-speaking lawyer who works in the company's legal department, were also in Islamabad. I was stunned. 'What? Ashford? Ashford's out here? I don't believe it. Oh, my God! The Taliban told me a high director had spoken with their embassy but I thought it must have been by telephone.'

David said the moment I was captured he was dispatched from Quetta to Islamabad to become a reporter/diplomat/fixer until Paul Ashford arrived. The news then got even better.

Salayha Hussain-Din had accompanied him to smooth through any cultural differences. She and I had very quickly become friends after the Richard Desmond take-over in November 2000. The legal department had moved into offices near my desk and Paul Ashford set up an office just opposite. The three of us used to do coffee and tea runs for each other.

I asked David about my family, because I was under the impression that my mother was somewhere in Islamabad. All the Pakistan officials had been talking very excitedly about her as though they had spoken with her personally. Little did I know she had become a great British institution overnight. I was to find out a lot more about her stunning media performances over the garden gate in the coming days.

David then introduced me to a very quiet, young man who was sitting in the corner. His name was Akbar Shinwari and he had worked round the clock with David, organising cars and security for my impending release. Akbar had even gone out and bought a burka, which was used by one of the photographers to lure the baying press away when we left the political agent's office. It was a good diversionary tactic but it fooled only some people into believing that the burka-clad person in the back of a car was me.

Colin Mulcahy arrived in a Range Rover and we headed off to Islamabad. Although I was very hacked off, he was an extremely endearing person and very disarming, which is why, I suppose, he works as a diplomat. As we headed towards the capital he said, 'I hear you were very difficult inside. Have you been in a foreign prison before? There are courses you can go on that guide you how to behave when you're arrested.'

I stated that I hadn't been to prison before and was wondering why he had inquired. This was the second time in two weeks I'd been asked that. I continued, 'If I'd been locked up in either Iraq or Iran I would have been on my knees begging for mercy, but these people were different. I tried to push the Taliban as far as I could because I needed them to think that I was the complete opposite of what they expect from their women. It seemed to work well and here I am. Hopefully, I'll be allowed to remain in Islamabad and continue my work.'

He told me there was no way I could stay: I had become a security risk because I was instantly recognisable. It was only then that it began to dawn on me just how massive the media treatment of my arrest and detention had been.

Just then his mobile sounded, and he handed it to me. Paul Ashford was on the line so I braced myself for a bollocking. He sounded exhausted, emotional, tired and happy. I apologised for being such a nuisance and then asked about circulation. 'Yvonne, this is not a time to be thinking about circulation. We want to know how you are. You don't know what you've put us through but we're so happy you're safe.'

I couldn't believe the warmth that came tumbling through that mobile phone. People get the impression that Ashford's a bit of a cold fish. Clearly he is not. He's very tall and lanky and has a beard, and when he wanders around the office he seems quite detached. He's also one of Richard Desmond's (the chairman's) right-hand men and so there are those who are naturally wary of him.

The clock was nudging 11 p.m., so we agreed to meet in the morning at the High Commission. As we arrived a film crew shot us driving into the compound where the Ambassador, Hilary Synnott, and his wife Annie were waiting to greet me. He asked me what I would like and I said, 'A large Scotch and a bacon sandwich,' then added, 'It's OK. I'm only joking about the sandwich. I'll wait until I get home.'

However, Annie turned out to be the perfect hostess and amazingly whipped up a delicious bacon sarnie. In the meantime, I finally got through to my mother's home and a strange bloke answered. I enquired who he was and it turned out to be Mark Blacklock, an *Express* journalist based in Newcastle. He had the job of 'babysitting' my mother to make sure she didn't fall into the hands of a rival publication. This was so bizarre.

Finally, I spoke to my mother, and she sounded so very elated and happy. I said I would speak to her in the morning. She said she had spoken to Daisy and Daisy had squealed with excitement down the line, and had then dropped the phone and had run off to tell all her friends.

Hilary was a superb host and he began filling me in on what I had missed. He then remarked that he had heard I had been 'extremely difficult' inside the prison and he'd been told this by the Taliban Ambassador, Zaeef.

Apparently Zaeef had told him that a representative of the British High Commission had to be at the border to collect me because 'she is saying very nasty things about us and you must stop her'. I laughed at the very thought that the world's most feared regime was getting upset because I had threatened to expose them. He, too, found it amusing and then added, 'I told them we can't gag members of the British press – I'm afraid I've got no control there.' Hmm, I think Hilary could have left the last remarks until I was safely out.

I took my holdall upstairs. David Smith had packed it when he had emptied my room in the Crown Plaza. Why are men incapable of packing bags? Anyway, I routed through it and there were a couple of things missing. Most notable was my Agent Provocateur perfume in a grenade-shaped pink bottle. I did not know who had taken it, but I wondered what they made of *that*. I had been accused of being a spy and someone must have gone into my room and seen this bottle.

I then dived into the shower and it was glorious. It was a *real* shower, no zinc bucket or cold water. Oh, joy! Everything was so clean and tidy and there were loads of smellies. I couldn't find my nightie, either, so I put on my Osama bin Laden T-shirt and slipped between wonderfully clean cotton sheets. I was in heaven.

The next morning I was up at around seven and went for a walk in the grounds of the British High Commission, which are beautiful. There was a lovely water feature on one of the lawns and a more private garden by the side of the house, which itself wasn't particularly inspiring from an architectural point of view.

The Synnotts have two dogs, and, as you already know, I hate dogs. One of them was trying to terrorise a cat, which had positioned itself out of harm's way halfway up a trellis. I gave the hound a wide berth but the damned thing decided I was more interesting and chased me back up the garden steps.

I was greeted by Annie, and she invited me to sit at the breakfast table overlooking the garden. It was a most civilised way to start the day. We were soon joined by David Smith, who wanted to work on his second part of my prison experience.

I had mentioned before that I had kept a secret diary. He wanted it, but I explained it was written for the *Sunday Express*. I asked him about the bottle of perfume and he said that he hadn't noticed it. But he then added, 'It was really weird going into your room and not knowing what was happening to you. The room looked dishevelled and the bed looked as though it had been slept in. The television was still on, so were the lights and there was a "do not disturb" sign on the door.

'I found your bag and passport but I couldn't find your Cartier watch in the room safe, which I was told to look for. The room safe was wide open. Then I discovered you'd actually put your watch in the hotel safe downstairs.'

I was really surprised by what he said. 'But David,' I said, 'everything was switched off when I left the room. This is really weird. It's awful to think someone's been through my things. I wonder if the Taliban sent someone round, because I gave the interrogators my room number and told them where my passport was.'

It was most disconcerting, but I did find out later that an Italian television crew had bribed their way into Room 109 to film the inside. The *Express* photographers had also been there, but the pictures I was shown bore no resemblance to how I had left the room. My contacts book was lying open, my bed looked unmade, the perfume was missing from the dressing table and I certainly did not leave a 'do not disturb' sign outside the door.

I didn't dwell on it too much at the time because there were other far more taxing things on my mind. But a chance remark and a sinister turn of events would bring me back to Room 109.

11

HOME

Later that morning I had a visit from representatives of the American, Australian and German embassies, who were greatly concerned about the eight aid workers from the German-based Shelter Now International charity. They wanted to know how their people were and what sort of condition they were in.

I was glad to be able to tell them that the German team of Georg Taubmann, Kathe Jelinek, Margrit Stebner and Silke Durrkopf were fine, as were the Australians Peter Bunch and Diana Thomas. In my opinion, their spirits were good and their amazing faith and belief in God was getting them through. The diplomats left, grateful for the news.

I then turned to the American Ambassador and said that Dayna Curry was also fine and well, but that I feared for the youngest of the group, Heather Mercer, because I thought she was vulnerable to her situation. I had been with the women for only a relatively short time and Heather appeared to be very bright, loving and giving. However, I added, her reaction to the day the U.S. spy planes were shot at concerned me and her fellow Christians.

'You've simply got to get them out of there because they're not going to get a fair trial and I don't think Heather can take much more,' I said.

I then made a drawing of the prison, outlining entrances and exits. I listed the shift patterns of the staff, the strength of the walls, the hollows in the wall. I even mentioned two wasps' nests. I gave the measurements of the courtyard I had paced out so many times before.

David Donahue, the American Consul General, listened intently and then thanked me. When I finished the briefing, he gave me the telephone number of Nancy Cassell, Dayna's mother, who evidently wanted to talk to me.

I don't know what happened to the information but I hoped that maybe a Special Forces team would zoom in and pull the aid workers out. The main snag was that Georg, the Shelter Now director in Afghanistan, and Peter were in a separate part of the prison and met up with the women only once a week. The men would almost certainly be killed by the Taliban if the women escaped and they were left behind – although Georg did appear to command the respect of the Taliban. It was one of those awful dilemmas, and, after President Jimmy Carter's disastrous attempt to release American hostages from Iran in April 1980, it would take a very strong, gutsy president to authorise such a dramatic rescue mission.

Anyway, I felt I'd done my best and all I could do now was pray for them. I went back to my bedroom, which had been set aside for Tony Blair's last visit to Islamabad. I saw Annie and told her that I had developed a really bad itch and I hoped I hadn't brought any fleas or lice into her home.

That woman was totally unflappable. Some women would have put you outside and dropped you in sheep dip, but not Annie. She didn't even raise an eyebrow and said casually that she'd get a nurse to pop around. She also revealed that she was a qualified counsellor and, if I needed to get anything off my mind, she would be more than happy to help.

Paul Ashford and Salayha arrived and there were loads of hugs and kisses. Salayha was wearing a shalwar khameez and she looked stunning. We went upstairs and chatted while I put on some make-up and then the nurse knocked at the door. She came in armed to the teeth with all sorts of creams, lotions and potions. I showed her my irritated skin, and she said it just looked like a heat rash. She then asked me if I'd been sexually abused. I replied in the negative – and with that she was gone.

I did seek Annie out later that day because I wanted to ring Dayna's mum, but at the same time I felt extremely guilty and cowardly and couldn't pick up the phone. I had entered Afghanistan illegally, been arrested, was abusive to my captors and got kicked out after ten days. Dayna, on the other hand, had sacrificed her life to live and work among the poor in Afghanistan and was locked up on trumped-up charges. 'Where's the justice in that?' I asked. 'If I was her mother I would hate me. I really can't make that call.'

However, I then reasoned, 'Yet if I don't make that call I am being a coward. How can I live with myself then, because her daughter is so brave?'

We talked it through and eventually I made that call – and Nancy Cassell was wonderful. I told her she had a beautiful daughter in looks and spirit and that Dayna still wore make-up and took pride in her appearance, even though there was nothing to do and no one to see and prison life was routine.

Dayna was special, I said, and oozed goodness and kindness. She made my day when I saw her using eyelash curlers and asked if I could borrow them. Eyelash curlers in prison – how cool is that?

Of course I wasn't telling Nancy Cassell anything she didn't know already, but she seemed to take comfort from my words, and I felt better as well. I told Annie later and thanked her for her wise words.

Gary Trotter, the photographer, turned up and took pictures of me in my England football shirt. It was all I had to wear at the time. I'd bought it on the night we had beaten Albania when England played at St James's Park.

He came back later in the day to say 'London' – in other words, the *Daily Express* – wanted me to wear something floral.

'I haven't got anything floral,' I protested. 'I don't *do* floral and I'm not wearing floral blouses for anyone.' Then I pointed out that I had no choice of clothes, anyway, and if he really wanted to take a new picture he should take off his T-shirt and I would wear that instead. He did, and I did, and I'm not sure if the pictures ever appeared.

I was standing in front of this old statue of Queen Victoria, which some previous ambassador had rescued from a village in Pakistan years ago. It seems perfect in every way until you look down. Poor old Vic has no hands. A passing embassy official said, 'Yes, it was a very well-kept secret that she was a bit of a shoplifter. One of the Taliban's first victims, I believe.'

The embassy staff told me they could arrange flights back to London via Dubai, so we decided to go. It was pointless my hanging around because I couldn't go anywhere: I was too well known and was therefore a target for any nutter on the block.

When we boarded the Emirates flight, Paul, Salayha and I were so exhausted that I think we all fell asleep before take-off. I was physically shattered and those two were mentally and physically exhausted.

Any plans Salayha and I had to hit the shops in Dubai Airport were knocked on the head because the plane was really late and our connecting flight was held until we arrived. We were more rejuvenated on this flight and Paul explained what he and Salayha had done to try to get me out.

They had collected enough evidence in the way of news-story cuttings, pay slips, and letters from previous employers to prove that I had worked as a journalist for 25 years. They then had all of this evidence translated into Pushtu and Paul arranged a meeting with the Taliban's deputy ambassador in Islamabad.

They had several meetings and I know they must have been impressed because the Taliban had mentioned it to me during an interrogation. Paul added that the Taliban had said that, if I didn't calm down and behave myself, I would never get out of prison.

'We were so close to getting you out but you were behaving very badly. I wanted to drive up to Kabul and tell you to shut up myself,' he said. But he admitted that the worst moment by far was the first night of the bombing when he thought the agreement to release me would be broken.

He asked me what I really thought of the Taliban and I said, 'It's very difficult because we know they're brutal and yet they treated me with kindness and respect. People won't like it but I have to tell the truth.'

He agreed, adding, 'No, people won't like it, but I have to say they were honourable. They gave an undertaking that you would be released and they stuck to their word. They came across as having their own kind of integrity. Richard [Desmond] gave me an open cheque to get you out but I knew right from the start that offering them money could cause great offence.'

He then revealed that *Paris Match* had contacted the office to speak to him because one of their reporters, Michel Peyrard, had been arrested in the Jalalabad area wearing a burka. He faced spying charges and his people wanted to know what Paul had done to get me out and whether he would do the same for them.

'Ah, well,' Paul sighed. 'Back to the office and the mundane business of shuffling papers. Life's not going to be the same again.'

As we touched down at Heathrow I felt very nervous. Home at last! I was wearing my leather jacket and had my old baseball cap planted firmly on my head because my hair was such a mess. The dye I had used had turned it into straw and it would all have to be cut off, I thought. I put my sunglasses on because I wasn't wearing any eye make-up and I looked shocking.

We didn't think there would be many media people to greet us but a pack had turned up, so I just continued walking and ignoring most of the questions thrown at me. I heard a familiar voice shout, 'Yvonne Ridley', and from the corner of my eye I could see Jane Dreaper, who had been a very tenacious trainee reporter in Newcastle. Now here she was working for TV. She looked fantastic and I wanted to give her a hug but I had to keep on walking until I got into a waiting Space Cruiser.

There inside was my sister Viv and we hugged and kissed. Then, as we pulled away she hit me over the head, and said, 'That's for putting us all through hell – and there's a queue of people waiting to do that.' Then I turned and saw Jim Murray, my news editor. He looked absolutely knackered and I felt really bad because I realised he must have been through his own hell.

As we drove Jim told me how on the Friday I was captured, he'd been sitting in the news conference and had commented, 'I haven't heard from Yvonne yet but she said she would contact me around noon. I'll just go and check and see what's happening.' He recalled that it had been a slow week and they were still deliberating over what to put on the first seven pages.

As he had walked down the newsroom, one of the daily people had called him over and pointed to a foreign agency report that said the Taliban had arrested a British journalist and there were unconfirmed reports it was me. He returned straight back to the conference and relayed the news.

The night editor, Dick Dismore, apparently said, 'Well, that's the splash and a spread sorted out, then.' He says he can't recall the moment but apparently others in the conference looked at him in a startled way. He is such a pro that I could actually imagine Dick saying it without emotion but without wishing to offend anyone, either.

Paul Ashford had been brought into the urgent deliberations and apparently had said, 'I wonder if she could get away with claiming political asylum.' He freely admits to saying that and I laughed. There's a gallows humour in this industry and sometimes real life is so bad that you have to resort to it as a foil.

As our driver headed towards the Lake District, where Daisy's school is, Jim continued filling in all the blanks from the past ten days.

'Yvonne, I know more about your private life than I ever wanted to know. In fact, you no longer have a private life. We had no idea you'd been married so many times. Then this Palestinian came out of the woodwork closely followed by an Israeli.'

He also said he'd heard from a variety of my contacts, including a man called Malcolm X.

'Oh, yes,' I said. 'He's one of the former Hereford boys. I have a few mates who used to serve with the SAS.'

'Yes, I know. Well, they all contacted me. Malcolm X wanted to put a team together because he said he knew where you were being held. Several other people made similar offers,' Jim added.

I felt really pleased and, while I was grateful for the services of the Tall Man with the Beard, as Paul Ashford is known, it would have been great to be rescued by a bunch of crazy ex-SAS mavericks. There were even some underworld types who wanted to go in. That would have been funny. A set of thickset heavies who look like the Blues Brothers charging in to take on the Taliban.

There was a lot of laughter and newspaper gossip in the car but I later found out that my arrest had really taken its toll. Jim had taken a phone call at his home on the first Sunday I had spent in Jalalabad as a Taliban prisoner. It was from a friend who told him, 'This is not good news, mate. We've just heard she's going to be beheaded, executed in the local square on Tuesday morning.'

The person on the other end of the line is normally well informed and he made the call out of the best of intentions, but I don't know how I would have reacted if I had taken that message. Another friend contacted Jim to say that the interrogation squad sent from Kabul to question me were, in fact, a torture squad. 'Very few of their prisoners live to tell the tale,' he warned in an email.

For the duration of my captivity Jim came off the desk and was running a 'crisis centre', where he was trying to coordinate information about me, both coming in and going out. They were very concerned that any details of my army record would leak or that the fact that I had been married to an Israeli would be reported.

I gather Rebekah Wade, like me a founder member of Women in Journalism, had to contact several editors and ask them to be responsible in their reports until I was safely released. Barbara Gunnell and Tracey McVeigh of the *Observer* and Helen Carter of the *Guardian* set about organising a candlelit vigil outside Downing Street for me, which was later backed by Women in Journalism.

Julia Hartley Brewer – GBH – hassled her political friends and contacts at the Labour Party conference, and I gather my uncle, Joe Mills, former regional head of the Transport and General Workers' Union, also pulled in some favours on my behalf. A variety of MPs wrote letters urging the Taliban to be merciful and release me, while both the National Union of Journalists and the British Association of Journalists did their bit too. When Jim told me about all this, I felt quite overwhelmed and moist-eyed. It was incredibly moving that so many friends and colleagues had been pulling for me and I felt humble and grateful beyond words.

On the international scene I understand the Palestinian terrorist leader Ahmed Jibril intervened and President Nursultan Nazarbayev of the Republican of Kazakhstan also applied pressure. The latter came about via a friend of mine, John Mappin, who married a Kazakhstan-born ballet dancer called Irina. Another mate, Ian Lynch, whom I worked with on Carlton TV, set up a website and email petition calling on 'British Prime Minister Tony Blair to put Yvonne's plight higher up his agenda and to take more effective action to bring about her release'. The wording on the petition continued, 'Yvonne was only doing her job as a journalist and reporting on the humanitarian crisis in Afghanistan when she was arrested.'

He had many other ploys up his sleeve but was contacted directly by the Foreign Office, who told him that creating all this publicity could backfire since the Taliban might think I was a very important person who could therefore be used as a bargaining chip – quite a plausible suggestion.

Jim Murray had me spellbound with the tales of my mother's daily briefings to the world's media from the garden gate of her home in West Pelton, County Durham. Any attempts by the Foreign Office to gag her fell on deaf ears and, as a result, she hijacked the headlines for ten days – slap bang in the middle of the Labour Party conference. Alistair Campbell, Tony Blair's official media spokesman, must have been seething at the thought of some County Durham pensioner stealing Blair's 'presidential' thunder.

While Blair had Campbell, Joyce Ridley had two spin doctors, Ted Hynds and James Hunt, who were working tirelessly on my behalf. They planned and executed an international media campaign via newspapers, magazines, television and radio to convince the Taliban I posed no threat and genuinely was a journalist. They set themselves a mission to keep my name and face in front of the world media spotlight while winning the hearts and minds of my captors. I don't know how much of an impact it had with the Taliban but it did no harm.

Ted Hynds is a wily old Fleet Street investigator and former *Cook Report* researcher who exudes the 'can do' attitude of a man who knows his job well. James Hunt is a formidable political media consultant whose friendly and easy manner has helped him serve a number of senior politicians and businessmen as a personal aide de camp. They are both old friends of mine and my heroes.

Within hours of my arrest they had presented my mother with a communication strategy to help free me. My mother tells me that it was a single telephone conversation, lasting no longer than ten minutes, that changed her opinion regarding the true level of political will the government were prepared to spend to try and gain my release. It was a very hypothetical discussion that she had with James, however, one she understood and acted upon immediately. James identified the problem as one of determinism versus political will. James and Ted's guidance was critical for her, as they had instantly recognised that the Taliban needed to be wooed.

My mother's words had to reflect respect for their religion and their humanity, if it existed. Ted stressed there could be no sabre rattling, none of the triumphalism of the Falklands and Gulf wars and no mention of the bombing campaign build-up. Ted and James opened up communication channels far and wide so that these words would be heard. And Joyce rose to the occasion. She may be 74, but my mother, a retired business-studies lecturer, was a human dynamo. My sister Jill provided her with all the moral support she needed throughout the 10-day ordeal. James said my mother captured the heart of the nation with her honest, simple briefings. And Sir David Frost, who invited me on to his *Breakfast with Frost* TV programme shortly after I was released, told me that I should be extremely proud of Mum, because she had become a great British institution.

My mother presented me as a devoted mother and loving daughter. 'Yvonne is a professional journalist, albeit with an adventurous streak, just trying to do her job by telling the world of the plight of ordinary Afghans.' It sounds trite. But it was a simple concept and basic ideas are often the most effective.

I have to say I was irritated when the Taliban told me that Daisy was in the newspapers demanding that they release her mummy. I knew my mother wouldn't have used her so cynically but James later explained she had to be 'utilised'.

Their first move was to capitalise on the fact that it was Daisy's ninth birthday during the week following my capture. Daisy proved to be trump card in the media campaign, as it was her personal plea for me to come home that touched the international nerve. Her appealing face appeared in more than 280 publications worldwide under variations of the 'I want my mummy back' storyline.

To keep the momentum going on the political front, a number of private presentations were made and James arranged for Daisy to write a personal letter to Tony Blair asking for his help. This plan was given legs when they discovered she had in fact written to him on two previous occasions. The first was when she was aged seven. She had written to ask him to stop the bombing in Kosovo, and she was delighted to receive a reply from Downing Street. Three days later the bombing stopped and her self-belief was amazing. Then, last year, after visiting the Dome, she wrote again to the PM when she heard it was to close. Her private letter mysteriously appeared on the global media stage for one and all to comment upon.

As I said before, my mother was the other key player in their plans. James and Ted coached her in the use of placatory sound bites intended solely for the Taliban. They arranged for a series of international television and radio interviews in which my mother treated the Taliban with respect and courtesy and avoided the pitfall of demonising them.

This set the pattern for the next eight days. They would start with an early briefing with my mother to discuss the theme of the day and by mid-morning they would have transmitted the new story and begun the endless rounds of phone calls to overseas media outlets. My mother tells me that throughout the day James would be constantly in touch, honing and refining the 'Yvonne Ridley Show' with the greatest effect. My mother was instructed to have three writing pads beside the telephone. Every incoming call was to be tape-recorded and entries were to be made into the television pad, radio pad or newspaper pad.

Unlike most running stories, where the subject is the main agenda, this one had James and Ted marching to a different drumbeat. From the start of their campaign their media output had only one aim: to persuade the Taliban to let me go.

The international press pack who had camped outside my parents' home also expected regular bulletins from my mother. She was coached by James and Ted so that nothing she said could be misinterpreted. Initially, there had been hope of a quick release. But the situation worsened when the Taliban started using the word 'spy'.

Ted later told me that my family's frustration with the poor efforts of the Foreign Office helped their presentation to the Taliban. He was able to voice my family's disillusion and loss of faith in my own government by promoting my family's reliance on the goodwill of my captors. But, without the star performance of one Joyce Ridley, much of their work would have come to nought.

Jim Murray asked me, 'Who is that James Hunt?'

I laughed and said, 'He's a man that casts no shadow. Don't ask.'

As we neared the Lake District I asked Jim to allow me to have a private meeting with my daughter because I did not want her 'utilised' again. I called the school to ask if it was OK if I popped in for an hour.

It was a magical moment. Her boarding house has magnificent views over Lake Windermere and as I approached the door I could hear lots of excited chattering and children's laughter. A teacher motioned me to go round the corner and as I did Daisy had just walked out of the bathroom. Her curly hair was damp and she had a fresh, pink glow on her cheeks. She saw me and came running at me, hurling her arms and legs around me. I carried her to her bedroom and we sat on the bed and just hugged. She then gave a couple of little sobs and I asked her if she was angry with me. 'No. I know it's your job. But how could you be so silly as to forget your passport?'

We talked for a while and I told her I was sorry I had missed her birthday. 'I did sing it to you, though, Daisy. I sang from the room I was sitting in.' She looked at me with those brown saucer eyes and said, 'I know. I heard you.' She then showed me her poetry book and read some poems she had written.

Her bedroom wall was covered in birthday cards and I asked her how it had gone. 'Fantastic. I got loads of really nice presents and everyone wanted to sit next to me. I think it was because you were away.'

An hour later, after more hugs and kisses and a promise that I would always tell her if I was going abroad, I left and said I would see her at the weekend. She smiled and went running off to play with her friends.

The Space Cruiser returned and we continued our journey to a remote farmhouse in Little Langdale near Coniston. Jim explained all the Ridley family would be there and I looked horrified: 'We can't remain under the same roof for more than ten minutes without rowing.' I was half joking.

It was great seeing Mum and Dad again, but I thought they both looked a little weary. My colleague Gareth Crickmer (son of Clive) had spirited Mum and Dad away from the hordes of waiting press the day after I was released. Scores of reporters sat outside an empty house for a good twelve hours before they realised the garden-gate briefings had gone for good.

My niece Bianca was there and so was my sister Jill with her partner Paul Bailey. Then Viv and I made seven. We had a nice meal in a pub near Coniston and then returned to the remote cottage.

I was eventually left with my two sisters and I have to confess we got plastered! We had a great laugh and then Jill brought me back to earth with a thump when she said, 'When you thought you were going to die, how did you think they were going to do it?' Talk about being blunt! Not even the hardest-nosed hack has asked me that one.

The next morning, both bleary-eyed, Viv and I struggled out of bed, and went to the kitchen. Dad was making bacon sandwiches – they are so tasty. I don't know anyone who can make something so simple taste so good.

Afterwards, Stuart Mason, the *Manchester Express* photographer, had me, Mum and Dad walking across fields for reunion shots. I think the plan was for everyone to go, leaving me and Jim behind to crank out the secret diaries for that Sunday.

'I told the Taliban I don't *do* squalor,' I protested. 'Well I don't *do* the countryside, either. Please get me out of here.' He could see I was not part of the green-welly brigade and if he wanted to get the best out of me we had to head for a city.

I hugged Mum and Dad goodbye and our party set off for Manchester. Excellent! I was given the presidential suite in the hotel and a computer was set up, and on the Thursday I began to write the full version of my diaries.

As I said before, I had written dates and notes on the inside of a cardboard box that had held a tube of toothpaste. I was not allowed any writing materials in Jalalabad but when I had got to Kabul the Shelter Now girls had given me some paper. I kept it hidden and wrote mini-notes, buzzwords, times and dates on it.

When I was moved I hid the paper and when I was released I stuffed my notes down my knickers, along with a letter Kathe had given me to send to her brother Andreas in Hanover. The toothpaste box was hidden in my bra along with other notes and pieces of paper.

By Friday afternoon I had knocked out twelve thousand words and the diary went across many pages in the *Sunday Express*, as well as into foreign newspapers and magazines in more than forty countries around the world.

Daisy arrived with her uncle, Bill Brown, and we all had dinner that night in the hotel. When we got back to my room, Daisy was very excited. She loves staying in hotels and we usually watch a film from our bed, but we were so exhausted that we fell asleep. The bed was bigger than king-size but she still crept over and cuddled into me. It felt so good and I realised just how much she meant to me.

The following day we had a slow start. I hate mornings. Daisy was bouncing up and down on the bed. She was truly excited because Bill was taking her to Blackpool to the funfair. I wished I could have gone because I've not been to Blackpool before and I know how much Daisy loves fairground rides.

Instead, Viv and I headed for London. As the car drove over Blackfriars Bridge I began to feel rather emotional and I thought I was going to lose it. 'Don't you dare start now,' warned Viv, and I checked myself. The sight of the old bridge, the 'grey Lubyanka', looming large was wonderful and there had been times when I had thought I would never see it again.

As I walked into the newsroom it was great to see all the familiar faces again. Judging from the expressions on them, it was obvious some my colleagues had thought they would never see me again.

Martin Townsend came over and I could not help but remark on his weight loss. 'We've been to hell and back,' he said. I then checked my email and there were more than four hundred messages in the system, most of them pleasant. However, there were three very unpleasant ones. I responded in a likewise manner and all three ended up in a newspaper diary page – funny, that!

My voicemail machine was full, too, and so I went through the messages and most were from friends and well-wishers. There was a nasty message from the fascist group International Third Position and it made me smile. 'Time to turn those Nazi bastards over again,' I promised myself.

That night in the pub there was lots of jollity and laughter. Even the manager of the Mad Hatter pub insisted I have a drink on the house, which brought feigned outrage from a couple of my colleagues. 'Bleedin' hell!' said cockney Stu Kershaw. 'She goes off for some two-week jolly to Afghanistan and gets a glass of wine. What do you have to round here to get a free drink?'

That weekend I started going through the cuttings that had been saved for me. It's not often anyone gets a chance to read their own 'obituaries', but I did. Former colleagues who were obviously not expecting to see me again wrote some moving tributes. The best came from Martin Shipton, who is the chief reporter of *Wales on Sunday*. There was another by John Sweeney, a freelance journalist, which was never published, but we can read it today. First, though, the Shipton piece:

> When I was told on Friday afternoon that Yvonne Ridley had been arrested in Afghanistan, I wasn't the least bit surprised. In the 24 years since I first met her when we were both trainee reporters in Northeast England, she has always been a risk-taker, often surviving by the skin of her teeth.
>
> I hope very much that her luck holds on this inauspicious occasion. Yvonne stood out among the trainees at weekend schools in the late seventies. Most of us were earnest young graduates who had come from various universities round Britain with high-minded ideas about journalism's 'mission to explain'.
>
> Yvonne hadn't been to university and wasn't interested in fancy media theories. She was training to be a journalist so she could find out unusual information, write about it, and have a lot of fun doing so.
>
> She was the wildest party animal, combining great personal charm with the ability to go completely over the top. She would stay up all night, drinking many hardened male drinkers under the table, ultimately leading them to a greasy spoon café for breakfast.

Her early career was spent at a variety of papers in the Northeast: the *Stanley News*, the *Northern Echo*, the *Journal* and the *Sunday Sun*. Newcastle became her domain in the eighties and she made it her business to delve beneath the surface, infiltrating that city's underworld as she researched stories about rival protection rackets and drug wars.

There were times when I went with her into that world, accompanying her as she mingled with people rumoured to be leaders of the local gangland. They seemed to regard her with fascination verging on affection, probably because she used her charm and made it clear she wasn't frightened of them.

In the late eighties she became interested in a story that had fateful consequences for her. Some years before a rebel without a cause from the Northeast called Ian Davison had joined the Palestine Liberation Organisation and been sent on a mission to Cyprus. Together with some other PLO members, Davison hijacked a yacht and killed three Jews, allegedly members of the Israeli intelligence service Mossad.

Davison was jailed in Cyprus and Yvonne was determined to get an exclusive interview with him. To gain access to him she had to liaise with the so-called PLO Embassy in Nicosia. Again her charm had its intended result and she got her interview with Davison. More importantly for her, she fell in love with a PLO colonel called Daoud Zaaroura, who left Cyprus and went to live with her in Newcastle. They had a daughter, Daisy, who will be nine on Wednesday.

Until meeting Daoud, who for a while anglicised his name to David, Yvonne had a turbulent private life. She had two broken marriages behind her, with several other unsatisfactory liaisons. Her work was her consolation.

For a time Daoud helped her to a new stability. He settled well in Newcastle, where he now works as chief executive of the North of England Refugee Service.

A highly intelligent and cultured man who once effectively commanded part of Lebanon during its occupation by the PLO, Daoud had a fund of stories to match Yvonne's.

Through Daoud's contacts, she secured an exclusive interview with Ahmed Jibril, head of the Popular Front for the Liberation of Palestine. When she was seven months pregnant she travelled to Damascus to ask him whether his organisation had been involved in the Lockerbie air crash.

Yvonne's relationship with Daoud was placed under severe strain when she moved to Cardiff in 1993 to become deputy editor of *Wales on Sunday*. Very shortly after she arrived the then editor was diagnosed with cancer and went on long-term sick leave.

Yvonne took charge of the paper. After the paper went to bed on Saturday night she would embark on the mammoth trip to Newcastle, where Daoud and Daisy stayed, returning on Monday afternoon.

In August 1995, Yvonne left Wales to embark on a new career in Fleet Street, where she worked on a variety of papers. Initially she had some bad luck, encountering male chauvinism and a disdain for 'provincial' journalists expressed by some of the more unreconstructed hacks.

She also experienced frustration when one news editor pooh-poohed the story she brought in about illegal arms sales to Sierra Leone. Weeks later she was asked to empty her notebook for the benefit of a member of staff, who had finally caught up with the story himself.

Over the past year, however, she has found herself a comfortable home at the *Sunday Express*, bringing in a series of exclusives that earned her promotion to chief reporter. Her relationship with Daoud sadly ended and after another broken marriage she is currently without a partner.

As on other occasions in her life, she has been prepared to disregard her own personal safety in pursuit of her work. She has been in tight situations before, but never one as tough as this.

Yvonne has demonstrated her resilience many times in the past. I very much hope she will soon be in a position to write up the biggest story of her life.

I spoke to Martin afterwards and he said he really never thought he would see or hear from me again.

Here, then, is the John Sweeney piece:

The Coach and Horses, Rae Street, Farringdon, is a far cry from a Taliban prison cell in Jalalabad but I'd bet a little bit of money that the chat right now will be just as good.

For one of the great story-telling stars of the Coach – a sunless oubliette favoured by journalists from the *Observer* – is currently a guest of the Taliban's pleasure in the aforesaid prison cell.

Yvonne Ridley was arrested by the Taliban while doing her job, for doing her job. She is a journalist through and through. If she is – as has been alleged – working for the British Special Forces, then I am a duck.

Yvonne, who hasn't been heard of for almost two weeks, was arrested while working for the *Sunday Express*. Her nine-year-old daughter, Daisy, hasn't heard from her for that time. Some people might think it crazy to risk everything to spend time with the Taliban.

But all reporters worth their tea and ginger biscuits have done daft things. My esteemed colleague, John Simpson, the BBC's World Affairs Editor, turned transvestite and donned a burka – the full-length dress complete with yashmak – to get in and out of Afghanistan. You might think that Simpson would make a poor version of an Afghan Mrs Doubtfire, and I suspect that you might be right, but he did it because the story merited the risk.

In my career – such as it is – I have pretended to be Lord Sweeney, a Chechen, an engineer, a zoo keeper, a theatrical agent and the President of Bophuthatswana. No, it's too long a story.

To get out of the siege of Dubrovnik I once hid in the ladies' toilet of a ferry. I had to cram my knuckles in my mouth to suppress violent giggles because I never knew before that even ladies break wind. Had I been arrested by the Serbs, well who knows what would have happened?

My friend Maggie O'Kane of the *Guardian* criss-crossed Bosnia on buses, pretending to be a simple housewife, and hid at the back, hoping that no-one would check out her passport.

Once, in 1990, seventeen people turned up at the border of Stalinist Albania for a tour of Illyrian archaeology. The seventeen included a theatrical agent, an architect and a fancy goods salesman: respectively me, Maggie and the cameraman from Sky News.

All good reporters take risks. Yvonne just got caught.

I got to know her well when we both worked on th*e Observer*. That fine newspaper, the world's oldest, has been in the story-telling business since 1791 and Yvonne is a hilarious raconteur.

She would sit in the Coach, surrounded by her listeners, and give you a breath-taking, gobsmacking, blow-by-blow account of the story that mattered or her latest clash with the boss class or her amazing love life.

She is from the North East and educated at, as they say, the university of life. No toffee-nosed smartypants, Yvonne. Sometimes, she was caught off-guard by some cultural reference. At the *Observer* there is a computer file called quotquot, which is a list of embarrassing overheards. You only ever get into quotquot if you have said something which is a bit daft. My favourite one on Yvonne goes like this: 'Yvonne Ridley demonstrates the advantages of not reading the *Sunday Times* culture section: "What's a butt of malmsey and why is it dangerous?"'

But quotquot only tells you the embarrassing stuff. Yvonne is as sharp as a butt of mustard, an acute observer and – cliché alert – one with a heart of gold.

I can hear her now, weaving a story, leaving the listeners weeping with laughter, as she described the cruel knocks of adversity and how she sidestepped them.

Observer parties are always a bit swanky. She once turned up at the book launch of a colleague with a man on her arm who is, perhaps, the most famous (and infamous) lover in all England.

Yvonne stole the show, a world-class character. When I first heard the news Yvonne had been arrested I winced, then smiled, then emailed one of her legions of friends, the *Observer*'s best night lawyer: 'I feel sorry for the Taliban.'

Let us hope that the Taliban come to their senses and release our colleague. In the meantime, it is important to remember why journalists do daft things. We want to tell the best stories. And the best stories are those that powerful people who do terrible things don't want told.

And so, Yvonne, if by some magic you might be listening to this from your prison cell in Afghanistan, you should know that all your friends know why you did what you did.

And can't wait to hear all about it. From you, in person. In the Coach and Horses.

Both are moving tributes, but I am happy to say that I have survived a terrible ordeal – and have been able to tell you all about it. This would have been the end of my story and my book would have had a happy ending – but for a sequence of events that has left me very sad and confused.

12

THE MAKING OF A SPY

Trying to get back to a normal life (although I'm not sure what *is* normal in my life) has been difficult because I feel there is still unfinished business. My arrest brought a halt to my work in the region, and my departure from Afghanistan, when it finally happened, was rapid. My exit from Pakistan was just as quick. I didn't even get to say a proper goodbye to Pasha.

It has been difficult to adjust because, while everyone knew what was happening in the media, there are ten days of my life that are missing and I'm still trying to piece together that jigsaw.

Some of the missing blanks were hilarious. There was the high farce when I read all the stories about my being a member of Special Forces. I found it amusing that the Taliban had told a press conference that I was in the Special Forces – it's pretty obvious that I'm not SAS material, especially when you think how many cigarettes I smoke! However, the spying accusations being bandied about by the Taliban were very serious and potentially fatal for me.

Humour in newspaper offices can be quite black and vicious at times and one of the main culprits for gallows humour at the *Daily Express* was a journalist called Anthony Mitchell. Ant had been furious when his secret wedding plans leaked out into the newsroom and became even more enraged to discover Greg Swift had been responsible for imparting this delicious piece of gossip to me. I had immediately telephoned the priest to get more information and for this, Ant never forgave us. While I was being held in Afghanistan by the Taliban, Greg Swift was covering the war from the Northern Alliance lines.

Apparently, there were ripples of laughter around the office as Ant said: 'All I need now is for Swift to be shot and my joy will be complete.' Nice one Ant!

In complete contrast to these entertaining anecdotes, after 10 days of being treated with respect and courtesy by my captors I was shocked when I got a black cab in London. The East End driver recognised me.

'You're that bird that got locked up by them Taliban people aren't you?' I nodded and he continued. 'Did they rape you?' I shook my head and then he added: 'It's hard to believe. If I'd been out there I'd have given you a go.'

I couldn't believe it. I think he thought he was paying me a compliment. 'Welcome back to civilisation, Yvonne,' I thought.

Some parts of the puzzle will doubtless be missing for ever and there are some pieces I wish I had never picked up and connected. For instance, at least one party entered my room in the Crown Plaza and removed some items, including the Agent Provocateur perfume.

Dennis Rice, who works on the *Daily Express*, told me when I returned that an Italian television crew had been in my hotel bedroom ahead of David Smith. But, from the description I was given, it seems someone else had been in ahead of the Italians.

It may have been undercover Taliban operatives in Pakistan or just another bunch of journalists. I had given them my room number because I had nothing to hide. No money or credit cards had been taken and my passport was where I had left it. My contacts book had been moved and some papers had been disturbed. Furthermore, my bed, which was made when I left, had also been pulled back and searched. As I say, I may never find out who went in and what the purpose of their visit was.

When I returned to my flat in London's Soho, Viv said she had had to break into it because no one knew how long I was going to be detained. She called a locksmith, who quoted around £70 to change the locks, but when he got there he did not expect to find two downstairs security locks and three more upstairs on the door to my flat, so Express Newspapers had to cough up almost five times the original quote.

Viv said, 'I've never seen anything like it. The locksmith worked like a surgeon, operating with wires and mirrors to gain entry. It was unbelievable. When he got upstairs to your flat door he again used some wires and clicked through various chambers to undo each lock. He told me you'd obviously lost your keys before, because someone else had been there and done what he was doing.'

I stopped her in her tracks and asked her to recount the story again. 'But Viv, I've been here just over a year and I have had the locks changed, but I've never locked myself out.'

That began to niggle me and I spoke to the locksmith but he could not point me in any specific direction.

Dennis also said the television channel had shown a picture of me, Daisy and Hermosh on a barge in Iran. I had to laugh at first, and then I thought of the consequences and wondered if the Taliban had seen the bulletins. Al Jazeera has a huge following and its apparent ease at showing interviews with Osama bin Laden has made it compulsive viewing during this conflict for many Muslims and millions of others. While TV is banned in Afghanistan, the ruling Taliban still managed to watch it.

I was furious because these people at Al Jazeera could have cost me my life. The Taliban do not mess around if they suspect someone of spying, and I could so easily have been hung from the gun of a tank and paraded around as a warning to others.

I called the chief editor at the TV station's Qatar headquarters and said, 'I want to know why you tried to get me executed. What made you run two bulletins trailing a much larger exposé and what made you suddenly stop running the bulletins?'

He said Al Jazeera had received some authentic-looking documents that heavily implied I was a spy and they decided to run with the story while the London end of the operation made several more checks. He asked me if I would do an interview and I agreed as long as I was able to clear my name and, more importantly, get sight of these documents.

Several days later I met the journalist Nacer Bedri at the offices of Al Jazeera, which are just off London's famous Carnaby Street. We talked and I could tell he was suspicious of me. After we climbed the stairs I was out of breath and said to Nacer, 'Look at my gasping for air. Do you really think I'm Special Forces or a spy?' He smiled, but I knew I was going to have to go a lot harder to convince him.

We sat down and talked and he showed me photocopies of documents that contained authentic information up to a point. Inland Revenue tax returns looked genuine, but my annual income had been exaggerated threefold.

They had the title deeds to my previous home in London's Docklands and a certificate showing that the house had sold for £500,000 and not £220,000. Nacer gave me a photocopy of an Israeli passport belonging to Husband Number Three, and it all looked genuine. Then he had a Mossad code number and ID card, which he claimed also belonged to him. These documents were said to have been found on me when the Taliban made their arrest.

'What nonsense!' I remarked. 'If I didn't take my own passport into Afghanistan why on earth would I take that Israeli's documents?'

Nacer smiled, then triumphantly pulled out a picture of me, Hermosh (still can't bear to use his first name) and Daisy on a barge. 'There,' he said. 'This was taken on a river in Iran when you entered the country illegally.' I gasped with disbelief and then remembered that, several days into my captivity, the Taliban interrogators had said they had evidence to show that I'd been in Iran.

Who the hell was trying to get me shot? I asked myself. Then I looked at the picture again and initially laughed, saying it had been taken in October 1998 in Stratford-upon-Avon. Then an awful feeling came to my stomach and I wanted to vomit. I remembered where I had last seen that picture – in my top drawer at my new flat in Soho.

I had kicked out Husband Number Three a couple of weeks after those pictures were taken and they weren't developed until later, after he had gone. So who had been in my flat? I then remembered what the locksmith had told my sister and I had this terrible feeling of unease.

Nacer was like a dog with a bone and he could almost smell my fears. He then said, 'We know the documents must have originated from an intelligence source. I was inundated with them but we didn't know if some were fake or not. The file was originally sent to Qatar, our head-quarters, and then they were emailed and faxed to me.

'It was a really thorough job. We also know that the Taliban intelligence had the same file. It was a very complicated situation and the aim was either to use you or frame you. Either way, the consequences could have been dire,' added Nacer.

Dire? I thought. That's a bloody understatement. Instant execution, more like. I called a few friends and contacts who belong to or are connected to this dirty world of espionage and ran this information past them.

'This has the hands of American intelligence all over it,' said my man in Whitehall. 'My God, if you had come home in a crate that would have really swung public opinion in favour of bombing those barbaric bastards. Still, I wouldn't take it personally, Yvonne,' he chuckled. He would say that, wouldn't he? It could just as well have been the dirty work of British intelligence, Mossad, or even another foreign agency, for all I knew.

Then I remembered a conversation I'd had with the retired Labour MP for Chesterfield, Tony Benn, after the BBC's *Breakfast with Frost* show. He had read my account of my time in Afghanistan in the *Sunday Express* and said it was a good piece of journalism.

'You've put a human face to the Afghans while the West has spent weeks trying to demonise these people,' he told me. 'It's so much easier to drop bombs on an evil regime. You have done very well.'

I was so flattered. Benn is one of the greatest peace campaigners of our time, a brilliant orator and a very wise politician.

Obviously if the barbaric Taliban had tortured and killed me and sent my broken body back in a box, or even performed my execution live on Al Jazeera, it would have provided a wonderful piece of propaganda for the West.

An Islamic cleric I consulted on my return added, 'If the Taliban had believed in the contents of the file I think they would have kept you as a bargaining tool. You would have disappeared into the mountains of Afghanistan because they would think you might have valuable information which they would need to extract.'

Thankfully, the Taliban's intelligence people were not that stupid, and so I think I can now tell you why I was released. I think the Taliban intelligence officers realised that their Western counterparts were trying to manipulate them and they didn't like it. So, to everyone's amazement, the day after America and Britain had blitzed Kabul with fifty cruise missiles, I was kicked out of Afghanistan after Mullah Omar signed my release on 'humanitarian grounds'. It was a two-fingered salute to the West from the one-eyed spiritual leader.

I didn't escape entirely unscathed, either. The Taliban said in a statement to the media that I had been difficult, rude and had a 'bad mouth' and I think they were just as relieved as I was when I crossed the border.

However, weighted against the evidence supplied by my newspaper, they realised I was a journalist and certainly not a secret agent. And they had made an Islamic promise to Paul Ashford that I would be free to go once that was established.

I had also made a promise that I am honour-bound to keep. I gave my word to the Taliban cleric who asked if I wanted to convert that when I returned to London I would study the Islam faith. The Taliban kept theirs and now I will keep mine.

I have already seen Dr Zaki Badawi, who is head of the Muslim College in London, a prestigious postgraduate institution for Muslims. He has offered to help me understand more about Islam and for that I am very grateful. It is indeed a fascinating religion and, like every religion, has its finer points.

If there is anything I have learned from this whole episode it is to be tolerant towards the ignorance of others. When I returned to England, certain sections of the media were prevaricating, abusive and even down-right vicious towards me. Female columnists sat in the safety of their ivory towers, polishing their nails, ponti-ficating about me as a mother, a journalist and a woman. Their bile was undiluted and their rabid rants would not have been out of place in the marketplace in Kabul on a Friday.

Unbelievably pompous invective flowed from pens in all corners of England and Scotland, with the exception of a few articles written by people who really know me. Even the waspish and sometimes downright cruel *Private Eye* sprang to my defence.

More than a handful of humourless women at the annual Women in Journalism meeting that I addressed on my return felt it was fine to 'stone' me verbally. It was then that I realised that some people, mainly women, really did wish I had been raped or tortured, or come home in a box.

'The Taliban treated me well and I'm grateful,' I told that meeting. 'Maybe if they'd pulled out my fingernails, electrocuted me, held me down in freezing baths, abused me with a red-hot poker, these particular women might have been happier.

'I know Afghan women are treated horrendously by the Taliban and I hardly think the Northern Alliance, whose human rights record is just as appalling, will treat women any better. But I cannot be held responsible for the way the entire female population of Afghanistan is being treated.'

One night I was particularly troubled by the spiteful criticism inflicted on me, and I called the media commentator and former *Mirror* editor Roy Greenslade, whom I have known for many years. I asked him what he thought of it, and how long it would last.

He said, 'Yvonne, much of it is down to commercial rivalry and the fact that you work for Express Newspapers. Ignore it.'

A few days later, when I was walking towards the BBC's Bush House, an Afghan woman came up to me and said, 'Thank you so much for what you have written. I am no longer ashamed to say I am from Afghanistan. Your stories have helped make us human again.'

Those few kind words were a real inspiration to me and I realised that it is pointless to allow the bitter feelings of a few angry people dictate how I behave.

I have also since realised that my detractors are very much in the minority. When I visited Belfast to address the Society of Editors conference less than two weeks after my release I was mentioned in a very moving speech by the RUC's Chief Constable, Sir Ronnie Flanagan, and over-whelmed when he called me brave and courageous.

When I came to address the conference I praised the many regional reporters who expose drug dealers and crime syndicates and regularly risk their lives to bring the news to the breakfast table. I also paid a personal tribute to the Irish journalists who take risks daily as they go about their normal duty, and in particular singled out Martin O'Hagan, who was gunned down in front of his wife after he had written a series of hard-hitting exclusives about Loyalist terrorists wrapped up in organised crime.

Martin was killed on the same day I was arrested and, while I commanded headlines throughout the world, his bravery and courage went almost unnoticed, written off by some as yet another sectarian murder.

After my speech, his northern editor, Jim McDowell of *Sunday World*, thanked me for my words and tribute to his journalist. I salute journalists like Martin O'Hagan, and may they long be praised for their determination to expose evil and write the truth.

Later, I was stopped in the streets of Belfast by ordinary people who wanted to shake my hand, and at the Europa Hotel a young porter came up to me and said, 'Britain is proud of you.' Two middle-aged ladies followed suit.

Ed Curran, editor of the *Belfast Telegraph*, who was hosting the conference, said, 'You know, Yvonne, life is never ever going to be the same for you again. I doubt if you will ever be able to work undercover, and you're going to have to reinvent yourself.'

I reflected on his words and I was sad, because this is a great job and I enjoy being the chief reporter of the *Sunday Express*. I'm not sure how I will handle the future but I have a message for my critics.

I have a sense of humour and I will continue to laugh. I enjoy a drink and I will continue to quaff champagne. I love life and I will continue to embrace it head on. It does not mean I don't care.

And, especially after my experiences at the hands of the Taliban, my faith in God has been reinvigorated and I will continue to pray and hope he listens.

Some say that it was the strength of their Christian faith that landed the Shelter Now International aid workers in Kabul Prison, where they were held for more than three months accused of trying to convert Muslims to Christianity. Personally, I think it was a cynical attempt by the Taliban's religious police to close them down, but what I also know is that it was their faith in God that got them through the experience.

After five weeks of bombing, the Northern Alliance moved forward and the Taliban forces appeared to crumble, having been devastated by the might of America's relentless air campaign. When they fled from Kabul, the retreating Taliban took the eight Christians with them, heading towards Kandahar, their stronghold.

'We were scared. We knew that if we ended up in Kandahar we would probably not survive,' said their leader, Georg Taubmann, an experienced aid worker who has operated in Afghanistan for sixteen years.

Their vehicle stopped at night in the neighbouring province of Wardak and all eight were locked overnight in a freezing shipping container. The next morning they were driven to the prison in Ghazni, 80 kilometres (50 miles) south of Kabul. As they were being locked up a bombardment by American jets was under way. When the bombing stopped, their cell door was thrown open and an Afghan with a rifle entered.

'We thought that was it, and they were going to kill us,' Taubmann said. Instead, the gunman beamed and said a single word: '*azadi*' (freedom).

After spending another night in Ghazni my former cellmates were dramatically snatched out of the area by three US helicopters operated by Special Forces. I know I had predicted a dramatic rescue by Special Forces, but certainly not on this scale. I was particularly elated to see that Heather Mercer had pulled through and my eyes glassed over when I saw pictures of her hugging her father, who had maintained his own vigil in Islamabad.

I had a sore head that day because I had, by happy coincidence, been in the German city of Cologne the night of the rescue with the director of Shelter Now, Udo Stolte, and Kathe's brother, Andreas Jelinek, and his wife Katja. We had appeared on Stern TV, voicing our hopes and fears for the aid workers, and speculation was mounting that they may be freed. But, as people involved in my case know only too well, it is dangerous to speculate because rumours abound in Afghanistan.

We left in a taxi for our hotel when Udo took a call and said, 'They're free.' That feeling of elation was magical, and I immediately came out with the only phrase worthy of special occasions, which my friends have heard so many times before: 'We must have champagne.'

We went into a piano bar in the hotel complex and I called the journalist/producer Theo Heyen to break the good news and invited him to join us. He had been like a cat on hot bricks throughout the show because no one knew whether the news coming out of Afghanistan was going to be good or bad. As it turned out, the only news was full of ifs, buts and maybes.

I gave a toast to absent friends and Udo, who was constantly being dragged away to answer media calls on his mobile, also gave a toast and thanked God. I really can't remember when champagne tasted this good – so we had three more bottles!

We then heard that the sixteen Afghan employees of Shelter Now International were also freed when the Northern Alliance forces entered Kabul on Tuesday. I told Udo that the aid workers had been told that their helpers had been executed. They could not believe the information, but they could not be sure, and prayed for them during their twice-daily meetings.

My mind swung back to my two guides, Jan Ali and Naqeev-Ullha, whom I last saw in Kabul Prison. I had been told they had been executed, too, and was devastated. Thankfully, I was put out of my agony less than 24 hours after the Christian aid workers had been released, when Pasha told me that the guides had also been set free.

'Madam, your guides are out,' he said. 'The Taliban drove them down to Jalalabad from Kabul Prison and basically said it's every man for himself. You are free if you can escape the enemy.' The words were music to my ears.

I and my newspaper had campaigned quietly behind the scenes for their release. It was a difficult time for me because I had spent ten days telling the Taliban they were not my guides, so when I was released I felt unable to take journalists into my confidence and tell them the full story. My fears were justified, because some of the reporting was spiteful and malicious towards me, but, more importantly, it could have jeopardised their lives.

They were reunited with their families, and, happily, I can also report that rumours of their torture were also exaggerated. Pasha added, 'They have been treated very well by the Taliban but they were told they would be executed if you turned out to be a spy. Everyone is very happy now.'

Sadly, not all of my calls to Pasha were this happy. Less than three weeks after my release, American bombs blasted the tiny village of Kama, in the Kama district, off the face of the earth. I will never forget that feeling when I heard the words, 'Madam, I have bad news for you. The Americans have bombed your village. Kama has gone and some of the people you met have been killed.'

Naïvely, I told him they must have been stray bombs that had accidentally hit civilian targets. 'But madam,' he protested, 'then they have accidentally bombed Kama three days running.'

I closed the line and a great aching sob erupted deep from within me. The woman who had sung 'Rule Britannia' so triumphantly on the night Kabul was hammered was now cursing the war. I had been to Kama and it had no military or strategic significance at all.

I called my mother and sobbed: 'Those bastards have bombed my village. Kama has been wasted, it no longer exists.' I called my news editor Jim and anyone else who would listen. I was grief-stricken.

I then spoke with Alan Simpson, the Labour MP and chairman of Labour Against the War. I told him about little defenceless Kama and its beautiful people. He was very supportive and outraged. He said what I had to say was of significance because I had no political axe to grind and did not belong to any pressure group against the war.

I was an eyewitness. Someone on the ground. A journalist who could confirm that the Americans were bombing civilian targets. I had an important message to give people and so I have since addressed many meetings, voicing my fears about the military campaign.

There is lots of unfinished business and I have to go back to Afghanistan. I have to find those people I spoke to in Kama and I pray that all my friends are still alive. I want to be mocked once again by the woman who boasted she could have fifteen babies. I want to see the young woman who had aspirations of being a doctor. I want to see the young man who also had ambitions for a medical career. I have to know if they are still alive. These people were a great inspiration and they are the future hope of a country that has been at war for more than two decades.

I have fallen in love with many countries and cities around the world and it has always been easy to explain why: New York is exciting; Rome and its cuisine are divine; Venice is breathtaking; Paris is so chic.

However, my heart has been stolen by Afghanistan, a wild, unforgiving country whose contrasts of people are reflected in its stormy history, politics and geography. The author Ahmed Rashid, who wrote *Taliban: the Story of the Afghan Warlords*, summed up the country perfectly in a small passage.

Many years ago a wise old Afghan Mujahed once told me the mythical story of how God made Afghanistan. 'When Allah had made the rest of the world, He saw there was a lot of rubbish left over, bits and pieces and things that did not fit anywhere else. He collected them all together and threw them down on to the earth. That was Afghanistan,' the old man said.

Whatever is drawing me to Afghanistan I will go again and I ask my editor Martin Townsend and my mother

Joyce to understand this and allow me to return with a free conscience.

You may have won the first battle to ground me – but you have not won the war.